A BOY,
A BURRITO,
AND
A COOKIE

A BOY, A BURRITO, AND A COOKIE

From Janitor to Executive

Richard Montañez

TATE PUBLISHING
AND ENTERPRISES, LLC

Published by Tate Publishing & Enterprises, LLC
127 E. Trade Center Terrace | Mustang, Oklahoma 73064 USA
1.888.361.9473 | www.tatepublishing.com

Tate Publishing is committed to excellence in the publishing industry. The company reflects the philosophy established by the founders, based on Psalm 68:11,
"The Lord gave the word and great was the company of those who published it."

Book design copyright © 2013 by Tate Publishing, LLC. All rights reserved.
Cover design by Allen Jomoc
Interior design by Caypeeline Casas

Published in the United States of America
ISBN: 978-1-62295-791-0
1. Biography & Autobiography / Personal Memoirs
2. Business & Economics / Personal Success
13.03.28

TABLE OF CONTENTS

PREFACE

I hope as you read these chapters in this book that you will all understand that this really isn't an autobiography, but it's really our story. Yours and mine. Because I believe that in these stories you will find yourself in one of these chapters.

First of all, let me go back to where it all began for me. I grew up in a small town in Southern California called Guasti. In that town, it all consisted of one industry: wine. I literally lived on a farm migrant labor camp, and this small town must have been no more than a couple thousand people, with only one small grocery store. My town was developed by two types of immigrants: Italians and Latinos. When the Italians came to Guasti, they saw that the soil was perfect for raising vineyards. So a few gentlemen back in the twenties and thirties immigrated to Guasti and began to plant vineyards. They also began to build housing for laborers. Of course, the Latino immigrants were already here, so they began to hire many Latinos to pick the grapes and work the fields and work in the wine factory.

The man who created the town was Segundo Guasti. He built the first elementary school in the town and the town's only government agency, a post office. It was the post office that made the town an official city. The grocery store wasn't much of a grocery store. It kind of reminded me of the grocery store from the seventies TV show *The Waltons*. That's the kind of store we had.

I am Latino, but my mom and my grandmother make excellent spaghetti and Italian food. And I always wondered, being Mexican, where they learned that. It didn't dawn on me until later in life that the grocery store only sold Italian food. So it wasn't by choice that my mom and grandmother knew how to cook Italian food, but it turned out pretty well for us. So that's where I was born and raised until we moved.

Let me start by saying that I wasn't old enough to have an impact on the Civil Rights Movement of the sixties, but I was old enough for it to have an impact on me. Here's what I mean: growing up in a town where everyone spoke Spanish and very few of us knew any English put us in a tough position, and then the law came into place where school segregation was removed.

I was bused to a mostly white school along with a handful of other kids. I remember that first morning going to my new school. I was crying, telling my mother in Spanish that I didn't want to go to that school. When she asked me why, I said because no one spoke Spanish. And she said it was just something that I had to do.

I remember getting on the bus, which was green, and I was wondering why I couldn't get on the yellow bus. The green bus was a statement to everyone who saw it that we were different. There was something different about us; we weren't like everyone else. At that young age, I began to take that on, being different.

So we got to school, and of course, I couldn't speak a word of English. And remember, I'm talking about the mid-sixties—there were no bilingual classes. Needless to say, I couldn't understand anything the teacher was saying.

So then came lunch and recess, a great moment for me. A sigh of relief. Then I went out into the lunch area. I remember pulling out my lunch; it felt like time stopped. All attention was focused on me. Every eye was looking my way. You probably don't know why, but some of you may understand. It was that they were looking at my lunch. It was because I had a burrito.

Now I know you all understand that we have taco stands, and everyone knows what a burrito is today, but let's go back to the sixties. Very few people had seen a burrito. So it wasn't the taco stand that introduced the burrito to the world; it was me and my mom! So there I was with this burrito and with everyone staring at me. I put it back in my bag and hid it. I remember I went home and told my mom, crying in Spanish, "Mom, make me a bologna sandwich and a cupcake like the other kids."

The reason I said that was because I didn't want to be different. I wanted to be like everyone else. I didn't want people staring at me. Why did I have to be different? My mother, being the marketing genius that she was, said no, and she made me two burritos. And she said, "Here's one for you, and here's one to make a friend with."

Well, that happened on a Wednesday. I went back to school on Thursday and shared one with a new friend. By Friday, I was selling burritos for twenty-five cents a piece. I learned at that moment that there was something special about being different, that there was a reason that we all just couldn't fit into the same box. There was a powerful reason why you and I don't look the same, why you and I don't talk the same. There is a reason for that. And in the third grade, which is when I believe this happened, I got a hold of the idea that there was something great about being different. That's the introduction for me, so let's continue on, and I'll tell you some more stories.

I learned at a young age that there needed to be a commitment even in the most undervalued tasks. What does that mean? You have to be faithful in the little things because it's the little things that lead to the big things. Here's another example. Again, I'm still in the sixties, in second or third grade. But I remember my grandmother calling me and telling me to take a cup of water to my grandfather who was working out in the fields.

The housing we lived in was made up of one-room apartments. Everyone slept in the same room. The bathrooms were community shared, like a large gym. The kitchens were across the hall from the apartments, also community style. Everyone put their name on their own refrigerators. It was really wonderful. Every morning I had breakfast with five to ten families. I never realized, like many of you, we grew up poor, but it was a fun poor. You didn't know you were poor until someone told you that you were poor. I had a lot of fun.

The vineyards were within walking distance; there was no carpooling to work. You stepped into your backyard, which was the vineyard, and you were at work. So my grandfather was only a few hundred yards away working with the other men and women in the fields. The glass of water that my grandma told me to take him was filled with ice cubes and looked refreshing inside a mayonnaise jar. So I ran and gave it to him. He looked at it, drank it, and looked at me with his big, sparkling eyes. He looked at me so pleased and refreshed after I gave him the water. Now that I'm older, I look back and it seemed like such a small task to take him that glass of water, but to him it was a refreshing moment. It wasn't a small task. So every day until I got older that was my job. But I never looked at it as a small task because for him, you have to remember the little thing was big. Always remember that it's not always a small task to the person on the receiving end. It was my first experience refreshing someone. I never dreamed that many years later I would find a career in making and selling refreshing Pepsi and Lays.

As time went by, I had so many different jobs in my youth. I quit school at a very young age. It is probably the only thing I truly regret. And I don't even like to tell people at what age I did quit school. But I had to; I could not speak English, wasn't going anywhere, and had to make some money. I've had some crazy jobs. I've killed chickens for a living and worked in a car wash. I've been a gardener. I've had great moments, like being twelve years old and waking up at five o'clock in the morning because there would be a caravan that would pick us up and take us to the chicken ranches in the mountains, where our job was to kill chickens.

Sometimes we wouldn't make it back home in time, so we would set up camp. I really loved these moments, being twelve years old, working with old men who traveled the country, and we would eat over open fires, tin can in hand. I loved it; even today, I love canned food. In the evening, some of the men would begin to drink, and I saw some knife fights, people trying to actually hurt each other. Being twelve years old, I didn't really have a fear seeing those fights. I just thought, as long as I wasn't getting hurt, I'd be okay. But for a twelve-year-old today, that would be a nightmarish experience. But again, those of you who lived through the sixties know what I'm talking about. You found ways to survive.

So I was working at a car wash, and a friend of mine told me that a company called Frito-Lay was hiring. And I remember going to Frito-Lay in Southern California and applying. They gave me an application, but there was one problem: I could barely read or write, so I had my future wife, Judy, fill out the application.

The first time I saw Judy, I was about twelve years old, and I can remember to this day the feeling I had inside. I knew then that she would be mine forever, and a few years later at sixteen, she became my girlfriend, and a couple years after that, we were married. The future job at Frito-Lay placed me in a good position to propose to her. It's amazing that if you believe in your dreams, they will come to pass. You see, in my dreams, I wanted a wife with the name Judy!

That day, I went right back and gave the application to them, and they hired me. In those days, background checks weren't in existence (thank God). I had nothing bad, just nothing good. I started that evening. I had to work the graveyard shift. I had to come back at eleven o'clock, where they hired me as the janitor. I remember sharing with my dad and grandfather that I got hired at Frito-Lay. The look in their eyes was like I just graduated Harvard. You see, it wasn't just a janitor position; it was a breakthrough for the Montañez family. It was a great accomplishment knowing my background, knowing that, well, I caught a break. I did, and I'm always thankful for that.

So I was working at Frito-Lay, and I was the guy who mopped the floor and took out the trash. Going back to being committed to the little things, I made sure that every time I mopped the floors, they sparkled. I made sure that all the trash cans were empty. I made sure that anything my boss needed, I got done. I made sure that he could count on me. It didn't matter what time it was or even if it was someone else's job. My attitude for work is something I learned from my dad and grandfather. Work hard and have passion, no matter what it is. There wasn't a lot that my father and grandfather could teach me academically because they had no education, but what they did teach me was values. If my job was going to mop the floors, it better shine. If I was going to rake the grass, there wouldn't be a single leaf left behind. And again I'm not telling you anything your parents didn't tell you, but here's how it was really able to help me.

One day the new CEO sent out a video telling all employees he wanted them to take ownership of the company. Wow, an invitation to act like an owner, including the uneducated janitor. For me, this was my moment to change my life, my second break. (We will look at this in a couple of chapters.) Remember, many times it's the giants that come into your life for the purpose of creating a revolution in it. Goliath never challenged David. His challenges were to the king and his top army of leaders. David saw this as his life-changing revolution, his break. Why not? What did he have to lose? The rest is history. You need to recognize the moments that have been orchestrated just for you. Know when the stage has been set for you; know your cues and lines.

At a young age, I learned a secret that was never intended to be kept a secret, but a few kept it to themselves. Listen. Here it is, young and old. This will change your life. None of us are born successful, but we are all born to succeed!

You see, most of the things that I've learned to use are not things I've learned in a classroom. I missed my opportunity there. That's why I think education is such an essential function for every child in this country. If you can get it, go for it. If you can't, don't worry. You'll still make it. I like to tell people I am the most brilliant uneducated person they will ever meet. So many things I have learned as a child in the outside classes of the world, things I was able to use as I started working at Frito-Lay. And I remember again because I mopped the floors like they had never been mopped, the managers began giving me more assignments. One particular one was that I was to weigh the entire product that fell on the floor through leaks. It was product that we threw away. Thank God for great quality programs that Frito-Lay developed. When anyone ever asked me about our quality, my response was always with pride. My quality was so good that what I threw away as trash, my competitor put in a bag (careful what you buy). So I weighed the entire product, and it turned out to be a significant amount.

My father was the type of man who could build anything. He was very creative. And I was blessed that I inherited the same attributes that he had. I didn't know it until I became older. So as I weighed everything, and at the end of the day I gave the report to the manager. It said it was a lot of trash. So I went home and began to put together a proposal on how to fix all the waste areas so that it wouldn't be waste. Actually, I spoke it and Judy wrote it; nothing like a team. And for the plant, it turned out to be a couple hundred thousand dollars' worth of savings a year. Now that's just one plant. Tie that into all of the plants around the country, and that's millions of dollars.

So I began to get invited to some different meetings, and before I knew it, the janitor was asked to join the savings cost improvement teams. That led to several million dollars' worth of savings, so what I'm trying to say is, again, to be faithful in the little things. People will notice *you* and will look at you. Especially if you're a young person. If you're someone who's younger in age, for us older adults, there is something great about seeing a young person taking out the trash and doing humbling things. It's like, wow, that person's going to be a superstar one day. Let me look at this person. You've heard it said you get promoted because of who you know. Well, that's not true; you get promoted because of who knows you. How do you get noticed? How do you get invited? You will never get invited to something big if you can't accomplish the little things. So for me, it's always about being faithful in the little things.

Your greatest discovery is self-discovery. When you discover your purpose, you discover your gifts. And when you discover both your purpose and your gifts, you discover who you are. Here's what I mean. I told you earlier that I don't have an education, that I missed my opportunity. I could hardly read or write when I started at Frito. And here I am today writing a book. But it took me awhile to understand and find out who I was. Then I realized one day that everyone is born with some type of greatness. We are all born as geniuses; we are all born brilliant. And it's over years that we begin to accept others' expectations about us, and we don't measure up to what other people expect you to be. That begins to place doubt in you. I'm here to tell you to remove that doubt that's inside of you because there is brilliance inside of you. There is a talent that only you can give, and you have to understand it; you are all brilliant. We are all geniuses.

What a relief it was when I found out that I wasn't really an idiot. Such a relief. What joy when I finally realized I was pretty smart. You may not be what an Ivy League school says is intelligent, but who's to say that they've cornered the market on intelligence? And I'm not picking on them. I'm just trying to say you've been created with a mind that's unbelievable. Everything that was ever created at one point in time was born in the imagination.

Now there are many great things you get with an education. But to those who don't have it, I want to talk to you for a moment. It's okay if you don't have it; there's still greatness in you. You can still achieve those goals; you can still change the world, but you have to believe it. So once I discovered who I was and what I was capable of doing, it just opened so many doors.

Having hope will give you courage. Here's what I mean. Let's go back to the sixties and back to our childhood. Now you know you need to go back there as many times as you can because there is a wealth of treasure stored in your childhood memories. Just think about all the things that you tried to create then. If you created them today, you'd be a billionaire.

So courage, let me tell you a little bit about how hope gave me courage. Again let's go back to the third grade. It was three o'clock in the afternoon; we were in school, and the bell rang. On Tuesdays, there were classes for after-school reading. And I remember there were two trailers parked outside school. One was for the white kids, and the other was for all the Latino kids. One particular Tuesday, I broke ranks, and I got out of my line and got into the white line. You should have seen the reaction from my friends. They were all telling me in Spanish, "Ricardo, get back. You're in the wrong line. You're going to get in trouble."

I have to tell you, when I broke ranks and got out of the line that I was always told to get into and got into the line that was so different than my line, the line I wasn't invited to get into, I've never experienced that type of fear in my life. When you look at me, you'll know my ethnicity; you'll know my culture. You'll know I'm Latino just by looking at me. So as I got into that line as a little boy, with fear I wondered as all the other white kids were looking at me wondering why I was here.

I saw the two white ladies—actually beautiful white ladies. I still remember their blue eyes. But fear got a hold of me, and I wondered what they would do to me as the line was moving forward. I wondered if they would notice that I was different, that I wasn't in the right line. I had fear like I'd never felt. But read these words: I had something inside of me that was greater than fear.

All those of you with fear in your life, I want to give you the antidote to that. Understand, this is a ten-year-old boy standing in line that he was told was the wrong line. And I remember I looked at my friends because, as this was happening to me, I had something greater inside of me than fear, and that was hunger. I was hungry. And I looked at my friends, and as they shouted, "You're in the wrong line!" I pointed to the front and said, "They have cookies inside. I want a cookie."

So as the kids began to walk in, I got closer. I walked up the steps, and there I was, face-to-face with these two white ladies. And you know what they did? They filled my pockets with cookies.

Now you are probably wondering what the moral of the story is. It's simple: hunger is the antidote for fear. There has been a cookie baked especially for you. Your job is to get out of that line you're in and get into the cookie line. If you're hungry, get out of the welfare line. If you're hungry for that new job, get out of the unemployment line and into the cookie line. When you're hungry for that one thing, fear won't stop you, as the pains of hunger are stronger than the grip of fear. Remember this: your own will will always try to pull you back, whether intentionally or unintentionally. No matter what room you're in, someone will try to steal your destiny. For me, my destiny was to meet those two beautiful women because they filled my pockets with cookies.

IF YOU WANT WHAT YOU'VE NEVER HAD, YOU NEED TO GO WHERE YOU'VE NEVER BEEN

Sometimes in order to achieve your goals and dreams, you need to go places you have never been. Again, let's go back to our childhood memories. Growing up on the poor side of town had many obstacles, but as I wrote, it was a fun poor. I can't really explain it. I guess many of us from the other side of town were like those wilderness survivalists. We knew what it took to survive. Anyway, one obstacle was crossing the tracks to get to the other side; we literally lived right next to the railroad tracks. During Halloween, a group of us would risk crossing the tracks to the other side; for us, that meant a dangerous adventure. Remember, we're talking about the sixties, a time when people stayed on their own side. But for my friends and me, we were willing to go where we'd never been in order to get what we never had. You see, on the other side of the tracks lived the rich people with the large homes, and during Halloween, they gave out the best candies!

Sometimes we would only get a few, as we were told to go back to our own neighborhood. Please understand, it did not hurt us; it just gave us more determination and added to the adventure. Sometimes you just can't take everything personally. If you can understand this, you will never again be hurt by someone's ignorance. When it comes to discrimination, there are two types. One is in the heart, and the other is in the mind. The one in the heart is the one you stay away from; it is a higher being's job to change that heart. The other is the one we can work with. Usually, the one in the mind just does not understand and can be changed with cultural education. For example, I never liked sushi until I tried it. Food is a great resource to bring people together. Remember my burrito story? After that, I became pretty popular, and everyone wanted to be friends with me. You should have seen the day back in the third grade when I brought a group of white boys over for dinner. My family had such great pride entertaining the white kids. For those few hours, we were all different yet the same. As I got older, my future wife, Judy, and me would cruise the same rich neighborhoods and wonder what it took to live there and how one got it. We would dream and let our imaginations run wild. Listen, it works, since without a dream you don't move.

I wanted what I'd never had. For me, that meant many things. Inside, I just did not know what would happen to an illiterate Latino kid from the south side whose gift was to sell burritos. One day, my wife looked at me from out of nowhere and began to tell me that I was a great man and that some day my gifts and talents would lead me to stand before great men. I thought, *What gifts? Selling burritos?*

One day I was walking downtown, and I saw an advertisement for some basic educational classes. They were being held in a church, and the teacher was actually a minister. I thought, *I never finished school; there is no type of educational system for me.* But I thought, *It's a church, they have to take anyone, and besides, it can't hurt to have God on my side.*

So I enter, and the minister, who today I consider a friend and mentor, invited me in and began to give me the lessons. As a few weeks went by, the teacher looked at me and said, "I see greatness in you." He had just returned my first-ever book report, and he gave me an A. For the first time in my life, I got an A.

Listen to what he said to me: "You have a spirit of excellence!"

Excellence in me—never had anyone spoken such a profound statement to me. Those words became like armor around me. Wow, nothing could stop me.

Today I realize that a mentor is more than a coach. Listen to this story of Mentor.

There is a legend about a Greek general, Odysseus, who was being sent to fight in the Trojan War. He was not sure he would return and was concerned about the welfare and raising of his son, Telemachus. Legend has it that the general asked his trusted friend if he would watch over his son. His friend responded with these words: "I will teach and raise him as my own son." The name of the general's friend was Mentor. This is where the word *mentor* originated. It originated from Greek mythology. Mentor was the name of a wise and faithful advisor of Odysseus (or Ulysses as the Romans called him). According to mythology, through Mentor's guidance, Telemachus became an effective and beloved ruler. Mentoring is a fundamental part of development where one person invests time, energy, and personal know-how in assisting the growth and ability of another person. Mentor's job was not to merely raise Telemachus but to develop him for the responsibilities he was to assume in his lifetime.

Now listen to this: a *mentor* is someone who can bring the unique combination of wisdom and skill together and apply it throughout an organization. I know that many of you are mentors. Whether it's at work, play, or home, you mentor. We win because of you. Mentoring is one of the best methods of encouraging human growth and potential…and it goes beyond coaching.

Listen: *stay away from those who discourage you; hang out with those who encourage you!* Mentors can see in you what you can't see in yourself and help bring it out. Each of us has the potential to be great—not famous but great because greatness comes by serving. In simple terms, mentoring is investing in someone the same way a parent invests in his or her own child. *Mentors can see the invisible in order to achieve the impossible.* Every accomplishment, large or small, starts with a decision. Choice, not chance, determines your destiny!

This was the first time I had ever heard words that made me feel like I was great, yet I never did anything great. (Oh, wait. My grandfather gave me a great smile after I gave him a glass of water.) What is a spirit of excellence here is my thoughts. The Greek word for *excellence* comes from the word *diaphero*, which means to differ, to test, prove, the good things that differ, to distinguish between good and evil, lawful and unlawful, to approve of things that excel, to excel, surpass oneself. The original concept or view of excellence encourages us to differ from others through the qualities of virtue and goodness, doing the best in common, everyday things with our given gifts and abilities, and using ways that build goodness.

The pursuit of excellence is striving to maximize one's talents. There is a big difference between individuals who are successful achievers and individuals who have an excellence about them. Individual successful achievement is commendable and needed in society, but excellence is something we can all achieve. Here's what I mean. Taking your gifts and talents to win a race is personal successful achievement. But when you use those same gifts and talents to bring and build a better place for all, that is true excellence.

In its earliest appearance in Greek, this meaning of excellence was ultimately bound up with the notion of the *fulfillment of purpose or function*...the act of living up to one's full potential. In ancient times, excellence was culture with courage and strength in the face of adversity, and it was to what all people aspired.

Listen, the word actually means something closer to "being the best you can be" or reaching your highest human potential. Excellence is not gender specific; it applies to all. Excellence is also frequently associated with bravery, but more often with effectiveness. The man or woman of excellence is a person of the highest effectiveness. They use all their faculties, gifts, strengths, bravery, and wit to achieve real results.

You see, the original concept of excellence is striving to be the total you. Excellence is not describing the fastest, smartest, or best looking in the room, so a person of excellence is simply one who strives to be the best they can be.

Excellence stresses utilizing those given gifts to the limit of your potential. A person may not be that intelligent, but if he utilizes his intelligence to the utmost limit of his capabilities, he is deemed to have reached perfection. Whereas the individual with far superior intelligence, who has authored many scholarly works, if his potential was even greater than that, and he could have pushed himself to the limit of his capability to become an even better person, he is deemed a less perfect person than the other fellow who did indeed utilize his capabilities to its fullest.

Creativity is a natural extension of our enthusiasm that shows up as excellence, and the way to achieve and maintain excellence is to deviate from the norm.

You know, my wife's words came true, and I have stood before great men. I just don't tell anyone since no one really believes me, but it's fun to know that I have had lunch with U.S. presidents, spoken at a special session on Capitol Hill, and been to the United Nations at another special session. I went where I'd never been in order to get what I never had.

Here is how I use it in the present. I learned that we all have two gifts within us: excellence and greatness. Our job in life is to find our opportunities to release our gifts in all situations. I began to believe there wasn't anything I could not accomplish. I began to attend plant cost-saving meetings and learned the systems that were important to our organization. Remember, I was still the janitor. The managers I had were great and received me and my ideas with enthusiasm, and together, we actually broke barriers between managers and front-line workers. I have to give a great deal of credit to the Frito-Lay training capabilities. Some of the best programs in the world are led by PepsiCo. Once I learned what was important to the company, it became important to me.

Sometimes you just can't wait for an invitation; just show up. I can guarantee your presence will add the missing link.

One particular day as I was writing one of my programs, I was doing it on a computer. For me, it was the first time I had ever been on a computer. Remember the little boy who broke out of the line into the cookie line? Well, here came the fear again, but thankfully the hunger for learning was stronger. As I was writing, I had a dictionary in one hand and was typing with the other hand, and in walked a young female manager who saw me and simply said, "Richard, you don't need the dictionary. The computer has spell check."

I was totally astonished and replied, "Wow, they can spell for you."

You see, the young lady was just not a manager. She was an angel sent my way. Look, that could have been a disaster with the wrong person walking in. That scenario could have looked like this: "Everyone, come look at this fool. He is using a dictionary with the computer." The wrong person could have had devastating results on me. I am a firm believer that there are certain people who will be sent into your life to help you find your purpose; your job is to recognize them. Don't miss them. And some of you are sent as someone's angel. How will you respond to the person who may look foolish? Will you teach?

You can take your current condition and use it to determine your future position.

First, let me speak to the young people who may be reading this book.

Young people, you were created with a purpose, given gifts and abilities that can't be duplicated and since the creation of time there has never been, nor will there ever be, anyone like you. Where others saw my disabilities, God saw my abilities. Where others saw what I was, God saw what I would become. My disqualifications were the very things God used to qualify me.

There are two types of ideas: evolutionary and revolutionary. Purposeful ideas are always revolutionary. In an instant, your life is changed. All ideas and inventions have not yet been discovered. Young people, concentrate on your condition and let purpose concentrate on your position. Here's what it does: it takes your current condition and uses it to determine your future position.

An idea would revolutionize my life and the company I worked for. My current condition was mopping floors. One day I heard our new CEO via videotape speak about taking the company and treating it as our own—again, a special invitation to be part of something big. Look, don't take your position for granted regardless of what that position may be. CEO or janitor, act like you own the company. And don't ever let anyone stop you, whether coworker or friend. It's your life. Live it. Again, you don't need an invitation to become great. It's your choice, and you also don't need anyone's permission to become great. No one owns the rights to greatness, although there are some who may think they own it. (I will save that for the next book.) Remember the cookie line. It was my own who called me back. Get this in you: there is always someone in the room who will try to rob you of your destiny. Someone will call you back or shout that you're in the wrong line. Break ranks; do the right thing for you and your family. I love the fact that when I did, I could look my children in the eyes every day and simply say that Pops took care of business.

Destiny. I believe that we all have the capability of being a genius when we are born, but somewhere along the line, the world starts to tell you that you're not or you can't be. I don't think you should ever let someone else dictate how great you can be. For me, destiny would be mopping floors at Frito-Lay. Here's what happened on a special day that revolutionized my life. That day I walked out my front door and into my neighborhood. My old neighborhood was pretty vibrant, food street vendors selling just about every food you can think of. There was one particular vendor that we called in Spanish the "elote man" or in English the "corn man." He sells this tasty delicious corn on the cob on a stick. Here is how he prepares it: First it is fully cooked. Then he puts on different ingredients. Your choices were of cheese, chile, butter and lime. It's an incredible combination of taste. Then it hits me. Wow! What if I took the same concept and applied it to a Cheeto...the rest is history. It's amazing what you can see by just taking a second look at something. Each of you should be looking now for your idea, it's in front of you. My giant was facing me, my destiny calling me out, my chance to change the course of my life, my chance to change the world.

Let's stop for a moment. You might be thinking, *Hey, what's the big deal? It's only a Cheeto.* No, my friend, it's more than that. I said earlier that food has a way of changing the heart. I felt if only the world could experience the things that made me happy and the things I enjoyed, maybe, just maybe, it would spark something inside others. Maybe the CEO and janitor can become friends. Maybe those who lacked a formal education might have a chance at creating history. Maybe someone like me with all my inadequacies might just have a chance. But more importantly, maybe every teacher out there would understand that those two beautiful teachers with cookies changed my life forever.

Two of America's greatest human beings, Dr. Martin Luther King and Cesar Chavez, gave their lives to change the laws of America, and with that, the heart of America began to change. Today, not only are we the greatest country in the world, I believe we have the largest heart of the world. Listen, maybe your giant is facing you at this moment. If not now, be prepared to see it when it does show up.

Back to the story. I decided to put chili on the Cheeto, and I took some to work the next day for my coworkers to try. No fear. It didn't matter what people thought. Hey, I was the first to introduce the burrito to the non-Latino world. Well, maybe not the first, but the first to my class. Everyone liked them, so I did what the CEO was preaching: acted like an owner. I called him up, not knowing you weren't supposed to call the CEO. His assistant was a visionary herself for even taking the call. She answered the phone in the CEO office.

"Can I help you?"

"Yes, I need to talk to the CEO. I have a great idea."

She responded, "Who are you, and what region do you run?"

You see, only senior vice presidents and general managers would call his office.

"None. I mop the floors at one of our plants."

She said, "Okay, the CEO will want to talk with you."

The CEO on the phone said, "Hi, Richard, I hear you have an idea for me."

"Yes, I invented some new products that you need to try. I believe they will sell."

The CEO said, "Okay, I will be there in two weeks."

I was happy as could be, not realizing what I just did was break protocol, getting out of the line I was told to get in and crossing the line to what most thought was reserved for just a few. Not true—the cookie line is for everyone. Sometimes you need to break out in order to break through.

Soon after my call, a manager walked up to me after he received the official call that the CEO would visit in two weeks.

"Who do you think you are calling the CEO? Do you understand what you have done? You're doing the presentation."

Someone's always in the room ready to rob you of your destiny. What had I done? I could barely read and write. I knew nothing about presenting an idea. My wife, always in her positive force, said we should go to the library and check out a book on marketing. Great. Check out the book and copy word for word how to create a marketing and sales strategy. Go to the plant and produce my own bags of product and design the bags myself. I didn't know until then that I was also an artist.

The day came, and the CEO showed up with his top senior executives. They were amazed at the product design, and I started my presentation wearing my three-dollar tie. (By the way, I still have that tie.) Everything was going great, and I was feeling it; then just like that, there was a question from one of the top marketers: "Well, Richard, how much market share are we talking about?"

For a moment, fear gripped me like back in the days of the sixties. I was ready to faint and for a couple of moments began to wonder what I was trying to do and just who I thought I was speaking in front of such great, educated, and talented men and women of the time. I was just the kid from the south side of town. Wow, market share. I thought, *Boy, I haven't read that chapter yet!* Then I remembered the size of the racks that held our products and our competitors' products and thought about the competition's rack and measured with my arms open to gesture the size of the racks.

And I said, "This much market share," arms opened as wide as one could with the biggest smile you would ever see. Can you imagine how ridiculous that statement was? But I was blessed with a CEO and vice president who took that line and repeated it.

The CEO said, "Ladies and gentlemen, do you realize we have the opportunity to gain this much market share?" with his arms wide open.

The vice president of sales, who today is the CEO of Pepsi Americas Beverages, Al Carey, stood up and gave the same challenge to the sales team. "Do you think we can get this much market share?"

And that is the day that led to the development of Flamin' Hot Cheetos.

It's one of the company's most popular items today. And I like to think that Flamin' Hot Cheetos and people like me and you help add spice and flavor wherever needed, and maybe just maybe, it changed how we see each other. I have had the opportunity to create many other products with great pride, but the one thing I am most proud of is the change it created in me and those leaders around me. The CEO and executives at PepsiCo looked beyond who and what I was at the present time and saw into the future and what I would become! Together, we started a change in corporate America, a change that says every employee, regardless of title, brings a value. In order to achieve greatness, you have to be willing to look ridiculous. Many times greatness takes on a ridiculous form. Just look at all the ideas that were thought of as crazy. Nothing can be more foolish than some of my ideas. There is also a good proverb that says, "He takes the foolish things of the world to confound the wise." Crazy ideas are sometimes the ideas we need.

I will always be grateful to PepsiCo for helping me discover my talents and gifts. They took the time to teach me the simplest things needed for success, the things you may learn from a university. Here is what you need to know: If you are the CEO, you need this and if you are the janitor, you need to know this.

Good leaders build talent…*but great leaders build people*! When the seeds of leadership leave your hand, it never leaves your life. According to *Webster's Dictionary*, leadership means to guide on a way, especially by going in advance. It is significant that the root of the word *leadership* does not have to do with power, command, and dominance. It has to do with going somewhere together with others. It is not so much about *being number one* as it is about "leading the way" through *one's own actions*.

In its truest expression, leadership is fundamentally about going first and influencing others as much by one's actions as by one's words. From this perspective, effective leadership can be viewed as the ability to involve others in the process of accomplishing a goal within some larger system or environment. Are you doing what you love?

Mark Twain said, "The secret of success is to make your vocation your vacation." In other words, love what you do, and do what you love! Leadership takes ordinary people and gives them power to do extraordinary things. What matters most is not what you do but how you do it.

You see, great leaders don't create the success; they help turn on the inner switch that leads the activation to a revolution in your life. But always beware: someone in the room will try to rob you of your destiny!

HAVING HOPE
WILL GIVE YOU
COURAGE

Having hope will give you courage.

Job 11:18, New Living Translation (NLT)

Hope is a powerful force. It's the fuel your heart runs on. It's the single biggest difference between those who finish and those who give up. You as a leader have this same ability. You just need to understand and believe it. Everything in creation is designed to function on the simple principle of receiving and releasing. Life depends on this principle. Plants release oxygen; others release fruit.

The tremendous potential you and I have been given is locked inside us, waiting for opportunites to be made on it. We owe it to the next generation to live courageously so the treasure of our potential is unleashed. The world needs what has been deposited in you for the benefit of the generations to follow. Do not dare leave this planet before you release it.

There is another old proverb that talks about vision. My people perish for a lack of vision. Vision is the source of life and hope. Helen Keller said, "The only thing worse than being blind is having sight but no vision." Dr. Myles Munroe says it this way, in his book *The Principles and Power of Vision:*

> The greatest gift ever given to mankind is not the gift of sight but the gift of vision. Sight is the function of the eyes; vision is the function of the heart and soul. Eyes that look are common, but eyes that see are rare. No invention, development, or great accomplishment was ever done without first seeing the vision.
>
> Vision is the key that opens the doors to what was, what is, and what will be. Vision sets you free from the prisons of limitations and allows you to enter into what the mind and heart can see. It is vision that makes the unseen visible and the unknown possible. [1]

Listen, vision reveals your destiny—and to reveal means to unveil.

Something that is unveiled was there all along but could not been seen externally. So as I continue to write, I am hoping that every teacher will understand that a cookie given with love can change the world. I hope that every C student will see that there is greatness already stored in them, and their job is just to simply believe it and release it. And I hope that every parent who has ever heard the devastating words, "Your child has learning disabilities and may never fully function like the rest," will realize that is not true. Have hope for your child; they were never intended to live like the rest. They are special treasures given as gifts to us. We are all brilliant human beings and all hold the gift of genius. Never let a test speak of who you are; we can't let others say being dyslexic is a problem or being mentally challenged is a setback. You see there, the ones who have been given special abilities and can see what we can't and people with special abilities can bring a revival into our lives and communities. I think people said I had every learning disability there is and some disabilities yet to be discovered and I should never had succeeded. We need to accept the fact that all are born with a purpose and bring contributions to this world. The only difference is some contributions may look more exciting than others.

We are all born to achieve something significant, and you are destined to make a difference in your generation. Your future is not ahead of you…it's in you. Purpose is when you know and understand what you were born to accomplish, and vision is when you can see it in your mind by faith and begin to imagine it.

Remember, you were created and designed to live in an environment that you influence rather than allowing your environment to influence you. You don't have to be a product of your environment; your environment can be a product of you! Even be careful of taking on an environment thrown at you, like a credit report. Bad credit doesn't mean bad people.

Back in 1969, we had the family car repossessed, and it was not funny or interesting, as the reality shows may point out. No, it was painful and embarrassing. My mom would take all us kids to the lot where the repossessed car was parked. We would look through the chain link fence with joy, motioning to each other and saying, "Look, there it is."

All of us would envision riding back in the car. Not sure how we did it, but with a few more cuts and savings, we did it, and we drove home in the old Ford. Here is what I am saying: let no agency ever place a label on you. There are times when we will all struggle, and get this in you: we are all first class, and there is no shame in living at or under the poverty level. It's your choice to be happy and to claim your spot in this world, not a credit report's choice!

I read this story somewhere:

In plain sight yet invisible at the same time.

In the 1950s, the Golden Buddha was discovered in the city of Bangkok, Thailand. For years, a huge, ugly concrete Buddha sat in the middle of town. Visitors put trash on it and never saw its value. Then one day, a priest decided to take the old statue to his temple. In the moving process, it cracked. As the pieces crumbled, the priest noticed something underneath the concrete shell. He gathered some helpers. They pulled the shell away, and inside they found the world's largest chunk of sculptured gold, standing around eight feet high. For years it had been there, but no one knew it.

Many of us are like this statue. The real value is inside, and many times it will take the movements that come into your life that shake and at times crack you, as it is after the shaking and cracks that the real you is revealed. When you discover your inner given gifts, your value and potential will always be successful. You may say this is all you have. In reality, God can take your this and turn it into that. "When I let go of what I am, I become what I am intended to be."

Let me close this chapter by saying that even with the lack of a formal education, I have been invited several times to give lectures at some of our top universities, but I won't mention their names. I'm not sure they want this known. I have also been privileged to speak at some of the country's top Fortune 500 companies.

One day during one of my leadership classes, I was teaching an MBA class—and remember, there is always someone in the room who will try to rob you of your destiny. A student asked me a question, and the question was which university I attended. I answered University of Guasti. The student asked where that was. I said, "It's somewhere you don't know and probably couldn't get in. It's a private school."

Of course, there is no such school. Then his follow-up response was, "Why don't you have a PhD like my other teachers?"

I looked him straight in the eyes and answered, "Oh, I have a PhD. You see, I have been poor, hungry, and determined."

A company's greatest quality is diversity. If there were two of you, one would not be needed. There is no one on earth like you!

YOUR PAST DOES
NOT DETERMINE
YOUR FUTURE

L isten, we can never allow our pasts to determine our futures. Here is my example from a few years back. One day I got a call from the governor's office of California asking if I would accept a state government appointment. First I thought it was a wrong number until I realized it was not a joke. Again, how can a kid who never passed a math test be part of a team working on economic development? The second thing I thought was, *Wow, a government appointment!*

With great joy, I decided to accept, and the appointment secretary, still on the phone, said, "Great. All we need to do is a background check."

"What? Oh, okay. Hey, can I ask you a question? Just how far back do you go?"

Was my past going to haunt me forever? Would I ever just fit in? Let me answer for you. One day I received a phone call from the CEO of PepsiCo, and he told me to meet him in New York so we could fly to Washington, DC, for a high-level dinner meeting with some of the country's top leaders from Congress, nonprofits, and business. Wow. I remember thinking, *It was just a few years ago I was riding in back of a truck with the lawn mowers as a gardener, and now traveling with the CEO of PepsiCo to meet with government officials. How does that happen, from the back of the truck to here?*

When I got to the airport, it was actually the first time I had been on a plane, so I took the first seat I could find. The treatment I received from the flight attendants, peanuts and snacks before the plane took off, was pretty cool. The feeling was great until the flight attendant asked to see my ticket, once she saw it, she quickly indicated to me that I was in the wrong seat. I was currently sitting in first class but my seat was actually in the back of the plane.

On the flight back to California, I felt such embarrassment and thought, *When will I ever fit in and start acting like an executive? When I will stop looking ridiculous?* I really felt terrible. Then a small inner voice began to speak to me these words: *Don't be concerned, it's not where you sit on a plane that matters or makes you comfortable, but where your heart sits is what gives you comfort. When your heart sits in the right place you will always have comfort in your life. The beauty is you get to pick the place for your heart.*

Mom, Dad, boss, CEO, you need to understand that we are not created to fit in but are created to stand out. When you find out who you are, you find out what you are. You were created with the intent of impacting this world in a tremendous way. When something created doesn't work the way it is supposed to, one of the first things we should do is go back to the manufacturer for the instruction of operations and repair. Once you discover its original intention and how it should operate and what you need to repair, the thing is brought back to its original intent. When you understand that you were magnificently created, it restores who you are. You see, there is a great difference between rebuilding and restoring. When you rebuild a car or piece of furniture, any new part will do, but when you restore an object, you must go back to the original creator for the original parts. And this is what great leaders do: they restore people to their original intent. Remember, you were created to stand out, and you may never fit in. Maybe you think you don't have what it takes. Listen, if I can make it, anyone can. As I said earlier, don't let a test determine who you are.

Often, people confuse motivation and inspiration. Success is a product of successive setbacks. What separates successful people from those who don't succeed? Is it motivation or inspiration?

The word *motivation* comes from the Latin word *movere*, which means to move. Motivation can be defined as an internal drive that activates behavior and gives it direction. To put it simply, the ability to move from one failure to another without losing energy and enthusiasm is known as motivation. Motivation comes out of external influence that encourages you either with ideas or with individuals while inspiration comes from within and with internal influence. Inspiration results in a feeling of excitement and well-being and a desire to get into action instantly without any prompting while motivation needs prompting and encouragement by others.

Motivation also means to "stir to action." On the other hand, inspiration comes from the word *inspire*, which means "to fill with noble or reverent emotion." In a nutshell, motivation stirs you; inspiration fills you. And that is one of the major differences between them. When we get a glimpse of the brilliance of our lives, we unleash energy and passion to make our time count, and we're on the path to a deeply meaningful life. Our past is simply there to support our future!

> In everyone's life, at some time, our inner fire goes out. It is then burst into flame by an encounter with another human being. We should all be thankful for those people who rekindle the inner spirit.
>
> —Albert Schweitzer

Mr. CEO, how will you respond when someone from the field calls your office?

I am thankful for those leaders who fanned the flame in my life.

INDIVIDUALS
BECOME LEGENDS

I finally realized that God just wants to show off in my life and yours. The word "character" comes from the Greek word *ethos*. It's used to describe the guiding beliefs or ideals that characterize a community, nation, or ideology. In some languages "character" is used as a term to describe a person who can engrave with a tool, and one who can leave a symbol or imprint on the soul.

The character of an organization is not defined by a mission statement. Company character is defined by the content that you put out, company character is defined in your creativity, quality, customers service ... and opportunities of self-development. In simple terms, people define the character of an organization. Leaders with character are the ones who can instill passion and direction in a group. Character leadership is in the cultivation of an environment that brings out the best and inspires the individuals or group. When character emerges in a crowd, many times it shows up as courage.

In every generation there comes the opportunity for the most unlikely individuals to become the legends that give us hope for a better future.

Look, you were created to rule your environment—versus allowing the environment to rule you. Everyone and everything on this planet was made with and for a purpose, including you. You were born with evidence that your life contains something of value which this world needs. Purpose needs to move in you before it can move through you. Greatness is not governed by reality. Reality is governed by greatness. You have been given an inner compass that will help guide you to your purpose and success.

The magnetic compass was invented in China around 200 BC for use by Feng Shui practitioners to "align" the forces of the earth to help them maintain balance in their lives. It was later in time that someone discovered it could be used as a navigational tool. The compass's original intent was to be used as a guide to fortune and success in life.

Listen, it takes courage to follow your inner compass. Courage is displayed at unexpected moments. What you do in such moments can change you and those around you. A compass doesn't tell you where to go, it's a tool to measure if you're going in the direction you've mapped. Remember success is courage and courage is success. Mother Teresa knew at the age of 12 that her calling was to the world. She first became a teacher in 1929 and taught until 1948. In 1950 she became a missionary. It took 31 years to reach the beginning of her calling.

When it comes to poverty we need a mentality change. The problem is not getting a person out of poverty, the problem is getting poverty out of the person. I remember recycling aluminum cans not because I was concerned with the environment. I was more concerned with my economy. I needed the money. Of course, today I recycle because I care about the environment.

Young people, this is for you. One of my favorite leaders is King David, he was most unlikely to become king. Yet when others saw a boy, God saw a king. David was the youngest son of a farmer from a small town. David was a young man who was not even acknowledged by the members of his own family, including his father. Even those close to him saw a nobody who would become a nobody. Yet, David became the greatest king in the history of the nation of Israel. Even when his own father did not see what he was capable of becoming God saw it, you need to understand that even if people like your own family can't see your true destiny, there is someone who does.

Samuel, the prophet, is sent to Bethlehem to anoint the new king. When Samuel arrives there, he commands Jesse, the father, to gather together all his sons. They came before the old prophet one by one. It is in this process that God makes known His choice for king. But his choice is beyond the obvious he does not chose the handsome, nor the one who's name means intelligent. He skips the tallest. These men are all what we would like to see in a leader. Anyone of them would have possessed requirements to rule as a king. But the one choosing is looking for different qualities, he's looking to give a chance to those who may not look like leaders. People who may look like the most unlikely person. This gives everyone a chance. You see, everyone, whether beautiful or not, is given the right to achieve success.

Now when Samuel ran out of leaders to choose from, he asked Jesse do you have any more sons. Jesse answered just one more, but he is out working tending to the sheep. Samuel quickly calls to bring David, and immediately when Samuel sees him calls, it was known that this is the one God has chosen. What I find interesting is while David's father and brothers are having a great time, since it's kind of a party, he was out working and caring for the sheep. The first step in becoming a leader is caring and serving people!

Sometimes all we need is a second chance. Here is what his second chance does: He takes our handcuffs and exchanges them for cufflinks. He takes our prison jump suits and exchanges it for a business blue suit. He takes us from the prison floors and places us on the palace floors.

I know that there are great people who may be parentless and never had the loving touch of a father, or maybe your father was not caring and could not see the tremendous value you bring to the world, but there is one that does care over you. Just the fact that you are alive today reading this book is evidence enough that you're not done, regardless of what your situation is. As the most unlikely to succeed in anything I have a great hope and challenge; the challenge to live my life and follow my destiny. And I know that, like David, I was not chosen on my outer attributes but more on what is inside. No I will never be the best player on the team, but I can be the best player for the team!

SUCCESS IS FIRST FAILURE...AND FAILURE IS FIRST SUCCESS

Our human desire and hope is that we astonish each other with some expected and unexpected opportunity. *Astonish*, as defined by Webster's Dictionary, means to paralyze, deaden, to stun, as by struck with a blow. In Latin, we are told that the "tonare" in astonish means thunder, so astonish is said to mean thunderstruck.

The word *stunning* is closely related to *astonishing*. When you look closely, you will see in one way or another we are all stunning individuals. Some of you every day leave us stunned and astonished by what you accomplish. You may ask how you will ever astonish anyone, how you will be like the next great famous person. You don't need to be; we need you to be the next you! Not failing in school would never have led me to the Cheetos line or the early adventures of my life working with some of the most interesting characters in the fields and mountains of Southern California. Not having an education has given me a great passion to help those who may not be able to afford a good education to the point where I have been able to create scholarship funds that have helped thousands of children from low-income communities or given away thousands of laptop computers to low-income kids. My hope is that every child receives the best education available. Look, if I can become an executive without an education, just think what you can become with an education.

Understand this: the treasures haven't been hidden from you; they've been hidden for you! The world needs what has been deposited in you. We are obligated to release the wealth to the world. Take responsibility for your ability. I remember one of my younger sisters (I had six sisters and three brothers) and I would go to the Newberry's department store a few miles on the north side of town. Newberry's had one of those old-fashioned diners where you get shakes and fresh popcorn or any kind of sandwich. Both my sister and I would be experiencing revival at the thought of what we were about to eat. When we arrived and ordered, we wouldn't even speak out our order; we would point to the astonishing pictures of the stunning food menu. It's time to revisit the things that brought you great joy, like a simple meal with a loved one.

What was also astonishing was the look on the waitress's face when I pulled out the cash to pay for the meal. Understand, this was 1966 and not something you would normally see, a nine-year-old buying his eight-year-old sister lunch with his own money earned by the rights every person has.

While on the subject of work, a couple of blocks down the street from our house was the local juice plant. The plant produced both orange and lemon juice. Every day, big trucks pulling trailers of the citrus fruit would roar down our streets to the docks for unloading. The trucks would pull in onto a lift that would tilt the trailers sideways, and the fruit would slide down small doors on the sides of the trailers onto the conveyor belts. The only problem is that the fruit would jam in the small windows. There's where I would come in. I would stand on the side as the drivers pulled in and would let them know that I could help them unload for a charge of $1.50 a load. Many would accept my offers, and many would not. I would jump into the trailers and make sure there were no jams. It was one of the hardest things I did, as I would be slipping and sliding, hoping I would not slide onto the belt and end up as someone's breakfast juice.

Listen, your job or career doesn't determine if you're a success or a failure, and I know failure can feel like a slap in the face. And when it keeps happening, it's tempting just to give up. But you can't; you must "get up again." Failing doesn't make you a failure; quitting does. H.E. Jensen said, "The man who wins may have been counted out several times, but he didn't hear the referee." Brooke Foss Westcott said, "Great occasions don't make heroes or cowards; they simply unveil them." My failures are many, but they made me who I am today.

The word *revival* is from the Latin and may be interpreted as "to live again, to receive again a life which has almost expired; to rekindle into a flame the vital spark which was nearly extinguished." The word *revival* is also related to the Greek word *refreshing*, which simply means proper recovery of breath, or in my case, Pepsi refreshing the world!

Henry Blackaby wrote, "The word *revive* is made up of two parts: 're' meaning 'again' and 'vive' meaning 'to live.'

Thus 'revive' means 'to live again, to come or be brought back to life, health, or vitality."

Look, regardless of what the economic experts may say, they don't speak for you. It's possible—you can enter into the first stages of experiencing economic revival in your life. Many of us are being awakened to our original intent and purpose. You might have been down to your last breath, but something or someone sparked the inner coals and fanned the flame inside. Listen, it's time to revive that idea, that brand. Revive the imagination.

IT'S THE INVISIBLE
THAT PRODUCES
THE VISIBLE

All great things are created from the mind. What you imagine and plan in your mind is the invisible producing the visible. And you need to know that nothing outside of you is bigger than what is inside of you. Are you prepared to release the limit placed on you and to see the unlimited potential we all have? Everything you will ever need to be successful with is already planted in you. There isn't anything you lack, no excuses. Your children have much greatness inside waiting to be activated. Our job is to help set their course and to create opportunity for them to experience the power they have regardless of what some test may say. Too many times the world's most acknowledged experts on management will indicate what is a leader and what is not a leader. Take the job-skills test. According to the results of test, there is no position of leadership for me. I remember the first time I took it. The person who gave out the test looked at me and made me take it again. *Oh, God, here I go again, failing the test. How do you fail a skills test?* Listen: be careful of what you expose your loved ones to.

There are three things that I was exposed to that changed my life. Apply this and you will be just fine.

1. Inspire. Someone inspired me. The word *inspire* simply means to breathe life into someone. You inspire them to believe that their dreams and goals can come true.

2. Encourage. Someone encouraged me. Encourage means to take courage and implant it inside of someone so that they are never the same. Courage is contagious. Remember this: Stay away from people who discourage you, and hang out with people who encourage you.

3. Remind. I was reminded of who I was and what I was. As a human being and as a living person, I was given seeds and gifts. Seeds to plant and gifts to give. It's the seeds of life that release the plan. It's the seed that seeks the nutrients to produce the fruit.

There is another old proverb that says as a man thinks he is, so he is. If you think you are brilliant, it will come. Another favorite proverb of mine is, "Life and death are in the power of the tongue." Careful how you use it—use to inspire, encourage, and remind.

Every generation brings a new awakening of intelligence. Allow yourself to be part of that generation; allow your children to be the persons who will spark a revolution of a new hope—a hope that says all kids are created to be successful and to lead in this world, not just a pre-selected few.

Your identity is a part of your destiny. Don't allow people or circumstance to change your identity. Don't run from who you are; in fact, you should run to yourself. Love who you are. When you love who you are, you gain confidence, and when you have confidence, it's your first step toward success. You see, we all want to be accepted versus tolerated, but when you gain confidence, it helps set you free from any limitations placed on you, and again, you don't need anyone's permission to become great. You are designed specifically unique, and your birth is evidence that you are needed. And you are never too old to resume your purpose. Nothing you have done can ever cancel your purpose, and everything you have experienced—good or bad—is a tool of the past that helps lead you to success. No matter what happens to many of us, we will always survive because of the fact that we have learned to use our past situations or experiences as a guide to success. (Even if I have to, I will sell burritos on the corner.) No shame in that game—work is work.

I can remember back in that small house on the south side of town there were many times someone on the block had one utility shut off for lack of payment. It happened to us many times, but there was community on my block, and we saw a way to survive. If one day you as our neighbor had no electricity, we would simply plug in extension cords from the house without to the house with. We would do the same with water and hook up the hose. Some of you are laughing and crying at the same time because you remember you did the same. It makes us laugh as we tried to hide the cords, and it makes us cry because it was hard. There's nothing wrong with growing up in humble beginnings. It teaches you how to survive.

Some of you moms on a daily basis made strategic decisions at the grocery store, like purchasing a certain brand of liquid dish soap because it would also substitute for hair shampoo. Or the time back in the third grade, wanting to impress the class with my slick black hair, I used cooking lard, or as we say in Spanish, *manteca*, to slick my hair back. It looked great. The only problem was the heat. You could fry an egg on my head! Mom, I am sorry for sharing your secrets. I know you did it for us!

There are hidden treasures all around us, and the map is in your imagination. Remember, as I said earlier, the treasures haven't been hidden from you; they have been hidden for you! Today, we have the ability to survive every situation we face, and someone out there has the answer to the problems we face globally. You have the idea on how to remove hunger; children hold the answers; the answer for the children that may be living in rough conditions and without the basic utilities, which no child should be without.

> Idea: From the Greek "idein," for "to see"; cognates with the Sanskrit "vid" (to know) and Latin "videre" (to see) and the English "wise."

You know things, and you have seen things!

There are many heroes we can all be thankful for—heroes like the teachers who shape our children or the heroes who wear military uniforms or the fireman and police officers who serve us on a daily basis. Danger never makes heroes or cowards; it only reveals them.

Then we have inspirational heroes in corporate America. Yes, I said corporate America. Many of the country's top retailers like Walmart, Target, Kroger, and McDonald's corporate hire from the local communities, and when you take a close look at their leadership, you find many who were at one time cashiers, stock clerks, or owners who used to flip burgers. Companies like PepsiCo, with values that promote community well-being, can teach our government leaders what it means to serve.

One of the greatest examples of servant leadership is the man they call Jesus. Here was a leader who was raised in the poor town of Nazareth or, like many of us, was from the other side of the tracks. He was never educated in a fine school, yet he took his product across the world to every corner more than two thousand years ago. Nazareth was located between the Sea of Galilee and the Mediterranean Sea. Jesus grew from childhood to manhood there. In his day, Nazareth had a bad reputation; much like many of our low income neighborhoods—just because its a poor town doesn't mean it has a bad reputation. As Jesus's reputation grew, the leaders of his day began to question him and where he was raised. A few wondered if anything good could come from Nazareth. It's almost funny to hear those words about a man who did nothing but good. But it drives home an important point: goodness isn't tied into a zip code! Good things can come from bad areas. Jesus was actually the first leader to take his product to the international market. And today the story is still taught. His book has sold more copies than any other book. Motivational speakers use his material.

His leadership steps to success were simple: inspire, encourage, and remind people that their destiny is tied into their destination. It's important to know where you are going. Take a look at his twelve leaders. Not once did he give them a skills assessment test. He just asked one question: Are you willing to serve? He called for leadership, and twelve answered the call. And these twelve men changed the course of the world.

The same call of leadership is cast out to all of us; it's just a matter of accepting the call to lead. No one willing to serve is denied leadership. Even when his twelve disputed among themselves who was the greatest, Jesus answered, "The one who serves the others or the least of mine." Who are the truly great? The word *greatness* was first used by the Greeks to describe the gods and a person who was of large soul and spirit. Greatness is the quality of being magnanimous: greatness of mind, elevation, or dignity of soul. A combination of qualities, in character, that enables one to encounter danger and trouble with tranquility and firmness, to disdain injustice, meanness and revenge, to act and sacrifice for noble objects, generous or forgiving, especially toward a rival or less powerful person. So the truly great are those who serve the least fortunate.

How can we rise to greatness without climbing mountains and crossing valleys? Whether we're rich or poor, young or old, male or female, we carry within us the seeds of greatness. Planted seeds are nothing more than potential, unless they are fed by soil and nurtured by the sun. So it is with our seeds of greatness. It is only after they are brought into the light and nurtured by positive thoughts and actions that they bloom.

The truth is that no one is insignificant unless they think they are. The message is clear: it's time to awaken to our seeds of greatness.

William Arthur Ward describes it this way: "Greatness is not found in possessions, power, position, or prestige. It is discovered in goodness, humility, service, and character." In other words, it is becoming someone you admire—not for fame or fortune but because of the strong inner desire that was given to you at birth. Why not unleash greatness of character to our lives? For when we do so, we add value to them. And when we have value, our life has meaning. We need great people, we need you to become great, and we need you to encourage, point the way, and show what is possible.

If you're anything like me, I was never anyone's first pick to achieve greatness. I was never picked to lead anything big. It wasn't until certain leaders took a second look that greatness began to take shape. For me, it was the minister/teacher who called into my life great things; it was the PepsiCo leaders who saw the value in people and who could inspire the outcast to excel. It was leaders who gave us all a common goal, some of the most brilliant CEOs I have ever met who gave us all at this company the inspiration and opportunity to deliver performance with purpose, the belief that doing good for business means doing good for society.

And finally, for me, the greatest leader and salesman I have ever seen is Al Carey, the CEO of PepsiCo Americas Beverages. Mr. Carey empowered every person within his reach, a leader with the courage to pick the unlikely guy at the end of the line or maybe the person left over from picking sides. I am not sure if there would be a book without these leaders. Mr. or Ms. CEO, take notice. You have the same opportunities in your respective companies—the opportunity to raise up prophets. You see, that's all I really am, a corporate prophet who knows how to deliver corporate profits. Prophets have courage like no other leaders. They can stand and lead where others won't. Courage is not the absence of fear; it's the conquest of it. It's doing what you've never done before in order to go where you've never been before in order to get what you've never had before. It's choosing to take the unpaved road, the hard path, because it's the right path.

I heard a pasttor once share this story: Leaders are like goldsmiths. One day three gold objects—the gold ring, the gold nugget, and the gold signet—began to argue among themselves who was worth more. The gold ring declared, "I am better since I was made for a rich bride."

The gold nugget said, "I am better since miners risk their lives to find me."

And the gold signet said, "I am better for I seal the messages of the king."

They argued all night and finally decided to ask the goldsmith. Each made its claim for being better, and the goldsmith listened carefully but said he could not settle the dispute. The ring grew angry and said, "Why not? You're the goldsmith!"

The goldsmith answered, "That's the problem. I don't see a ring, a nugget, or a seal. All I see is gold."

Leaders have the unique ability to maximize the minimum and get the most out of the least. Some people live for a statement while others live as a statement. Don't limit your possibilities to the visible. Don't listen only for the audible.

Don't be controlled by the logical. Believe there is more to life than meets the eye! You are gold.

All young children test as geniuses in almost every way. But over the years, the slow accumulation of self-doubt, shame, and resistance convinces us that we are less than our true selves. Very often geniuses are so advanced that the society of their day rejects their ideas; their status of genius is usually confirmed by future generations. But the brain of the genius is unusually sensitive to lifestyle and habits and more aware of inequalities of the environment.

A genius is just someone who sees what others can't. Chances are, you are a genius with world-changing ideas waiting to come out. Keep in mind that as a genius, many times your ideas may be taken as ridiculous. The difference between successful leaders and those who are not is not in ability but in mentality. Nothing outside of you is bigger than what's inside of you. Here's a secret: it's the invisible that produces the visible; all things are created first in the mind. What you plan in your mind is the invisible producing the visible.

Keep thinking the impossible and the ridiculous. If you think only about sensible ideas and search only for the perfect idea, then you may fail to come up with anything new. The route to genius does not lie on the often-traveled path. Keep deliberately thinking of truly ridiculous ideas. This thinking opens up and awakens your mind to explore and find new answers.

You are a great leader, too. Read the words of on of the greatest poets. Marianne Williamson says it best.

"Our deepest fear is not that we are inadequate. Our deepest fear is that we are powerful beyond measure. It is our light, not our darkness that most frightens us. We ask ourselves, Who am I to be brilliant, gorgeous, talented, fabulous? Actually, who are you not to be? You are a child of God. Your playing small does not serve the world. There is nothing enlightened about shrinking so that other people won't feel insecure around you. We are all meant to shine, as children do. We were born to make manifest the glory of God that is within us. It's not just in some of us; it's in everyone. And as we let our own light shine, we unconsciously give other people permission to do the same. As we are liberated from our own fear, our presence automatically liberates others." [2]

Remember great leaders take their disabilities and turn them into great abilities in order to achieve great possibilities.

Even in a bad economy, most of us are still better off than others and better off than we have ever been. We may lack the latest, the biggest, the finest, and the fastest, but we seldom lack the necessary. Helping others is an obligation not an option. The truth is, we've been called to feed, shelter, and clothe the needy. In America, we are blessed over every nation in the world. We are the only country in the world where storage units are a billion-dollar industry. We even have reality TV shows on storage. People living in other countries make purchases out of survival needs. Here in America, we buy things that go into our storage. I'm not making a judgment here, just trying to make a point of how blessed we are. I am sure there is something in your storage you could give as a gift to a single mom or a struggling student or a homeless person!

———◆✦◆———

Anticipation is a wonderful emotion. It literally has us looking forward not backward, focusing on the possibility of good things to come. Anticipation is a central motivating force in everyday life; it's the normal process of imaginative anticipation of, or speculation about, the future. I learned there is a true value in understanding anticipation.

Back in the little town of Guasti, we finally moved out of the one-room projects and down to the south side of town known as the barrio. Wow, what great anticipation all us kids had. Just think: an eight-hundred-square-foot home with three bedrooms and a bath inside the house. That was more than enough room for us eight kids and Mom and Dad. Dad, like many men born in the thirties, was a master at building, and our home became a beautiful house. Several years later, I came home and found my mom in tears and asked her what was wrong. She said the sheriff had just left; we had lost our home and we had twenty-four hours to move out. I was shocked. After all my father did to the house after the years of paying the mortgage, we lost it?

You may have heard the term "homeless but not hopeless," but I don't believe you can understand until you lived it. In walked my father, who said, "Let's start packing." And as my younger brothers and sisters were crying, this giant of a man (even though he was five six) began to tell us there was something greater waiting for us and it was time for someone else to be blessed by this house. With that, my father gathered us all in a circle and prayed that the new owners would enjoy the house.

What great anticipation. We did not know where we were headed. Eventually, we split everyone up, and the kids went with different relatives. This was until somehow my father ended up with a two-and-a half-acre ranch with all the animals that come with a typical ranch. Today I still don't know how he did it, but I do know he had anticipation for the future.

Creating anticipation is a worthwhile job for all leaders, designers, and innovators whether they're creating content for traditional purposes or new innovations. Here's why this emotion is so important: anticipation leads to engagement, and engagement leads to activation.

Who do you look to for inspiration in your daily life? Who influences you and your profession the most? Who is your role model? For some of us, it may be our parents, and at other times, it can be past legends.

Recent scientific studies show that everyone is gifted with virtually unlimited potential for learning and creativity. Most of us perceive creativity as something acquired through practice and schooling. That may be true in some aspects, but it's just one approach toward learning and crafting your brain and developing your creative skills.

Many believe creativity is given at birth, and only those who are born with it are able to pursue it while the rest of us are left to wonder how to obtain it.

A genius is an extraordinarily intelligent person who breaks new ground with discoveries, inventions, or works of art. Usually, a genius's work changes the way people view the world or the field in which the work took place. In other words, a genius must be both intelligent and able to use that intelligence in a productive or impressive way. A great leader is a genius who can create optimism in the face of destruction, as my father did. Even though he lost the mortgage, he did not lose his courage and creativity.

Look at the word *mortgage*. It's a word that gets our attention. The history of the actual word *mortgage* is very interesting. In the word *mortgage*, the "mort" is from both the Latin and French word for death, and "gage" is from the word that means a pledge or to forfeit something of value if a debt is not repaid. So mortgage is literally a dead pledge. It was dead for two reasons: the property was forfeit or "dead" to the borrower if the loan wasn't repaid, and the pledge itself was dead if the loan was repaid. Another interesting fact is that the word *mortician* has roots to the word *mortgage*.

Many times we may feel as though there is a mortgage on our purpose. Understand this: mortgages have no legal binding on your purpose. You have a value and worth that can never be mortgaged, and as leaders, we face many situations and circumstances that require us to navigate through.

You can compare great leaders to our greatest world structures ever built by man. As a friend of mine once said, "You need to go deeper in order to go higher." When you look at the world's tallest buildings, you will see its beauty, but there is a beauty you don't see that makes what you do see possible. And that's because of the foundation. The higher you go, the deeper your foundation needs to be. So in the case of great leaders, it's their foundation that you can't see that reveals the beauty you do see. Like every great structure, its ability to survive the elements of the world is what makes them great. Earthquakes, hurricanes, and tragedy will shake at every foundation, and its ability to withstand these external forces will determine its greatness, not its outer beauty.

What you don't see in the foundation is the cost of going deeper and the lives lost in the building process. If you're reading this book, chances are your foundation has already been tested and has survived the elements. We lost our house but not our foundation. We went deeper, and today, we stand higher!

If you find that mortgages have been placed on your purpose or maybe somehow the morticians of life are trying to place a deed on your real value, you need to "put back in what was taken out of you." So refuse any mortgage placed on your future success. You already have everything within you needed. Never forfeit. Take back the interest paid on your dreams and reinvest in you. You're worth it.

Remember: your optimism is courage!

<hr />

Every organization needs champions. They're the greatest source of survival.

And they come in different forms and levels. Champions don't have a specific outer look; sometimes they look like moms driving the school bus or ministers visiting the sick.

I have had the privilege of meeting some of the world's everyday champions. Champions who are not famous but are know. Together, we have been able to feed several hundreds of thousands of families across the country in cities hit hardest by the down economy. There's nothing like handing a box of groceries to a family in need and seeing the smiles on the children's and parents' faces.

I have learned with success comes responsibility—a responsibility to our fellow citizens and humanity. The success I have gained was never really about me. It was about putting me in a position of influence to help support those in need.

I do appreciate our government. Even with its issues, it's still the best in the world and keeps us safe. But as successful leaders, it's our duty to help our fellow man regardless of what Washington does.

Today my family runs a not-for-profit organization called Onelite. Our mission is "Going where others won't and where others can't." What we do is we bring hope to low-income communities by providing groceries, new shoes for kids, backpacks full of school supplies, and even free haircuts. Typically, we hold an event every four months, and several thousands of individuals show up. Our events are always a success because we know whom we are serving. We know what it's like to receive an eviction notice, we know what it's like to stand in the welfare line, and we know what it's like to stand in the food line. As I said at the beginning of this book, when you have experienced hunger, there's not much to fear. We do all this in a way that brings dignity to those receiving. Remember, it's important for your success to really know whom you are serving.

My main two reasons for writing this book are to buy more shoes for kids and to inspire those forgotten by our society, those who have been told they will never be champions.

The original meaning of champion is not the same as today. The earliest meaning of champion was being a fighter or a combatant. From Latin, a champion is someone who went out on the campus. But to those old Romans, a campus wasn't where young men and women went to university; a campus was a field and, more specifically, a field of battle. An arena was also a campus, and sometimes the line between sport and battle was a little fuzzy for the Romans. So a champion wasn't necessarily the person who won the fight or the sporting event. It meant anyone who participated in the contest on the field.

Their mere participation conferred on them honor whether they won or lost. In simple terms, once we arrive and engage in the arenas, we become champions! We also know that gladiators were called in Latin champions.

Most champions also have intuition, the ability to see any event, from a viewpoint as a whole, from its culmination— the seed, the flower, and the fruit in relation to the whole; the knowing of something without prior knowledge or the use of reason. Intuition can be a comprehensive grip of the principles of universality. A person who develops intuition can know anything regardless of what obstacles they might face.

The intuitive type: creative people, people with hunches whose chief concern is with future possibilities.

History is filled with champions who made the decision and entered the campus and changed our world—champions like Mother Teresa and Rosa Parks, who led and became examples for us.

Champions aren't made in gyms. Champions are made from something they have deep inside them— a desire, a dream, a vision.

—Muhammad Ali

COMPETITION:
THE BREAKFAST OF
CHAMPIONS

There have been many defining moments in my life and in the lives of great human beings that changed their lives forever. These defining moments often set the course for the future of their lives. There can be more than one, each pointing you down a path of purpose and success. The secret of a great life is often a person's ability to discern the defining moments given to him/her, understanding them, and learning to walk in the path that leads to his/her ultimate destination.

Theodor Geisel, the great author and illustrator, had a tremendous impact and influence on me. When I first read two of his famous intellectual books, they actually helped define my life's course: *The Cat in the Hat* and *Green Eggs and Ham*. Geisel, known as Dr. Seuss, wrote forty-eight books that have sold well over two hundred million copies and have been translated into multiple languages. His first book was turned down by many publishers. Finally, a publisher saw what others couldn't and published Geisel's first work.

There are times when we may be turned down, and sometimes it just takes the right leader to see what others can't.

Here's to the crazy ones, the misfits, the rebels, the troublemakers, the round pegs in the square holes— the ones who see things differently. They're not fond of rules. You can quote them, disagree with them, glorify or vilify them, but the only thing you can't do is ignore them because they change things. They push the human race forward, and while some might see them as the crazy ones, we see genius, because the ones who are crazy enough to think that they can change the world are the ones who do.

—Jack Kerouac

Are you crazy enough to believe you can change the course of your life? When you look at people, do you see possibilities? There are many average individuals waiting for the opportunity to move beyond ordinary into the life of extraordinary. Can you see the treasure coming out of poverty? Many treasures are stored in dark places, and it takes a special kind of eye to see what others miss.

If you look up the word *craft* in dictionaries, you might see this: craft is a secret form of knowledge, locked away in some secret place known only to master craftspeople. Craft is taking technical knowledge and applying imagination. In all craft activity, there is making close contact with materials, technical skills plus imagination, sometimes pressure pushing at the outer limits of normal function. In fact, before a stone becomes crafted into a diamond, it's just carbon put under millions of pounds of pressure.

You don't have to be a world figure to have a dream. The pursuit of a dream is open to all. It's the difference between being ordinary or extraordinary. Ordinary people become extraordinary when they release their dreams. You also need to understand that releasing your dream many times will help release other dreams. One of the greatest individuals of all time had a dream of freedom, and when he released it, other dreams were achieved. A dream will inspire you to make needed changes in your life.

Size doesn't determine significance. Your dream doesn't have to be big; it just has to be bigger than you. Permission to pursue your dream comes from one source, yourself. Someone said, "It's never too late to become what you might have been." Rather than always focusing on everything, learn to focus on what is really important: you. You're important.

Many of the world's most successful craftsman/craftswomen were at one time considered to be just dreamers. Many laughed at Alexander Graham Bell when he dreamed about the telephone before it was created. There is a story of a woman who worked at a tortilla factory who is credited with playing an important role in popularizing the tortilla chip. In the late 1940s, she was employed at a East Los Angeles-based Tortilla Factory, and began making tortillas by machine, but at first many of the corn and flour tortillas were misshapen and had to be thrown away. This woman took some of the rejects home for a party, cut them into triangles, and fried them. They were a huge hit with her guests, and she began selling them for ten cents a bag. When others saw rejects, she saw opportunity.

Crafting is an ancient practice that is perhaps as old as the human civilization itself. Archaeologists over the years have conducted excavations in different parts of the world discovering various handmade objects of craft from different ages. Crafting reflects the culture, tradition, and history of a place and lives long after the culture has undergone modern transformations.

Look, everything created has a step-by-step protocol, and sometimes you need to break out in order to break through.

Creating history is just a matter of seeing and pursuing what others can't and won't.

Leaders are like jewel craftsmen. Diamonds are quite ordinary at first glance, and their true beauty as jewels is only realized through the cutting and polishing process. Cutting a diamond requires specialized knowledge, tools, equipment, and techniques because of its extreme hardness. A diamond craftsman takes imagination, art, skill, and science in changing a diamond from a rough stone into a beautiful gem.

———————————

I read this story:

Many years ago, a large American shoe company sent two sales representatives out to different parts of the world to see if they could develop some new business among the residents.

Some time later, the CEO received telegrams from both salesmen.

The first said, "Bad news. No business here. No one wears shoes."

The second one said, "Great news. Much business here. No one wears shoes!"

We have a choice for every situation: we face the choice to stop or the choice to move forward. I remember as I began to do well in my career, not everyone was happy for me. It was hard for many to understand why I had such a positive attitude about every situation that came my way. Again, if you've never really been hungry, it's hard to understand.

There is a word in Spanish, *ganas*, that has several meanings. It means passion, strength, and win. You need passion and strength in order to win.

A few years back, I taught a leadership class in my home. The class consisted of college students, and I called it School of the Prophets.

I used the name School of the Prophets because much of my material was just that—that of past experiences. Leaders today have to be prophetic. They need to have vision, to be able to see into the future. Prophets are the best at developing and calling out future leaders. Prophets have the gift of seeing where the treasures are stored; they can lead people through rough territories.

A note to all CEOs: You may have thousands of prophets working the front line, prophets making critical decisions on a daily basis. Why not empower them to look into the future? The future is already here; it's just a matter of releasing it. We know that words are a powerful source of energy. Like the old proverb states, "Life and death are in the power of the tongue."

My friend and leader, speak life into your people, speak life into your teams. Teacher, you have the most important task second to the parent. It's you who can enhance children's belief in their abilities. My biggest regret in life is never having the opportunity to attend school and earn a degree. You may say it's not too late, and you're right. It's never too late to learn, but for me it's just not the right time.

Looking back on my childhood, my family moved out of Guasti into a small town called Ontario, California. It was a place I really loved. It had all the makings of a small town, and the highlight was always the Fourth of July parade. There were marching bands, fancy cars, and free orange juice for everyone, donated by the local Sunkist Company. No one needed to wake me up on that day! I left earlier than anyone and walked the three miles. I did not want to miss the free orange juice. The parade always inspired me, and I can recall telling myself that someday I would lead a parade. I have learned that many times what you call out in the present is a release into your future. That was in 1964. Fast-forward several years to 1995. It was the Fourth of July, we just moved into a new city, and we weren't yet familiar with the local area. My youngest son, Michael, alerted me early in the morning, "Dad, we have no fireworks!" I immediately jumped out of bed. We couldn't let that happen.

So we hopped in the car and began to drive around in the new town. As we drove, we came across some roadblocks. Not knowing the area, I decided with caution to cross the roadblocks because it looked more like someone just forgot to remove them. I finally ended up on the main street, and in that town it really was the main street. As we drove north, my son and I both noticed that there were several hundred people standing on the curb waving to us as we went by.

My son said, "Dad, look what's behind us!"

I took a quick look into my rearview mirror, and to our amazement, it was a parade, and guess what—we were leading it. Talk about a rush of embarrassment, but hey, the people waving didn't know the situation. I quickly made my way out onto another street; then I heard a small inner voice, the same voice that had been with me for many years: *Richard, your dream came true.* What joy I had! You may think, *Oh, that was just a mistake.* But sometimes in order to achieve your dreams you may need to cross the roadblocks placed before you. Now please understand, I don't mean that you should literally cross roadblocks like I did. I mean it more as an analogy. And remember, not every mistake is bad!

Over time, we will face roadblocks for our safety and roadblocks placed just to keep us out. You have to be able to discern both and know when to cross with caution. For me, roadblocks began to appear at a young age. No, you can't go that way, not that way either. What can take an uneducated boy from the south side of town and today that same person is recognized as the "Godfather of Hispanic Branding," a title that was given to me by the media and others? It's because I figured out that many times the roadblocks placed in life were there to direct me to a certain path, so understand that many roadblocks are good for your destiny because they force you to turn a different way.

It's the same with the experts of life. Experts will say, "No, we can't do it that way. No, it will never sell." Don't be such an expert that you no longer can see new things.

Mom and Dad, no need to worry; your child is going to make it. Hey, if I can, anybody can!

YOU DON'T LEAVE
A LEGACY, YOU GIVE
A LEGACY

When you look at the word *legacy*, most would say it means "what you leave behind." But the true meaning of the word goes further than leaving something. Its original intended use was more of a legal term referring to a personal will and was meant more of what you give of value. The word is derived from the Latin "legare," meaning "to give by way of a will." It is a great value parents would give to their children or someone they cared about. A legacy is something that is given to another. Each one of you has a legacy

A community servant was once asked how he felt about people taking advantage of him and his kindness, and he replied, "I give my advantage away every day; it's not taken."

Now when you combine the word *legacy* with the word *extraordinary*, you enter a class into which few have ever stepped. The word *extraordinary* comes from the Latin words *extra*, meaning out of and "ordinem" meaning order. The adjective "extraordinary" surfaced in English in the early fifteenth century and originally meant unusual or out of the ordinary—in other words, people out of order or away from the norm. Extraordinary, gifted leaders many times speak in a tone that is out of key with the rest of the crowd.

How do you become extraordinary? Simple. Put extra on your ordinary. Remember, your extraordinary is not in your greatness. Your greatness is in your extraordinary.

Lack of courage quite often is traceable to a lack of extraordinary situations (danger). It is danger that brings forth courage.

Someone once said, "Life will never give you courage… but rather the opportunity to be courageous!"

Back to the story of David and the giant, Goliath. What is interesting is that the giant's challenge was not given to David; the challenge went out to King Saul, who happened to be the greatest warrior in his camp. But as great a warrior as Saul was, fear kept him from accepting the challenge. Why, you ask, would such a great warrior not accept this challenge? Especially since history and legend has it that Saul was the tallest person in the land, including all the battles he fought in. Yet this was the first time he faced someone or something bigger than himself, and fear grabbed him when he wasn't the tallest in the room.

You may not be the tallest, smartest, or strongest person in the room, and others may see you as marching out of order, but when challenges come your way, it is those who have a courageous desire who accept these challenges. And by accepting these challenges, you receive the same opportunity as David, the opportunity to create an extraordinary legacy, a legacy you can give to others.

It takes extraordinary courage to step out and volunteer to help teach a child with special needs, courage to step down and lift up a homeless person, or to cook a hot dog for someone who is hungry. Don't wait to leave a legacy. Start today to give your legacy.

Once again, a big thanks to all the men and women who serve our country in all functions: military, peace officers, and the fearless firemen and rescue workers who run to danger when everyone else is running from it. A special appreciation to the teachers who carry cookies and to the CEOs and executives around the world who release all their employees to achieve greatness regardless of backgrounds.

To my company, PepsiCo, for looking beyond the ordinary and seeing the extraordinary.

But special appreciation goes to every parent who never gives up on the child! You're the true leaders.

Remember, extraordinary courage can take a life no one else can use, and use it like no one else can!

On my third invitation to the White House, it was to be part of the official welcoming of Pope Benedict XVI's visit in 2007. Now, I am not promoting any religion above another, but what I would like to share are just a couple of observations I witnessed.

A few weeks before the event, I had to fill out the government background check, and again made it through. Your past many times may never give up; the past will try to remind and rob you of your future, but after this book, it will no longer have any kind of hold on me and, hopefully, for you as well.

I remember as I began to share with some of my friends about my future visit, I was amazed at the response I was receiving. So many thought it to be a wonderful opportunity! And I wondered why and what purpose this was meant for. It has to be more than just to meet the pope, one of the world's most influential leaders. It was not until the day of the actual event that I realized what the purpose of my attending would be.

As I walked the streets to the White House security entrance, it was incredible to see the people who lined the streets. I saw license plates from all over the country, and as I got closer to the security entrance, a couple of small eyes caught my attention. I looked down to see an elderly woman in her late eighties. As both our eyes met, she began to speak to me with in a voice of compassion. It was a look and sound I will never forget. Her words: "My son, tell the pope we love him." As she delivered those words, tears began to trickle down her wrinkled face, and soon after, I began to feel tears down my face.

That's when it became evident to me. I was not there for the celebration at the White House. I was there to see the multitudes of individuals who drove, flew, and walked across this country in the hopes of a glimpse. There it was: hope in the eyes of people. It was the hope of the pope! The small voice spoke to me. Look, people need hope. Give people hope for tomorrow, and they will cross any mountain. When people have hope, neither poverty nor the face of death can keep a person from reaching success.

Back in the sixties, at the age of twelve, one of my jobs was working for a company that maintained chicken ranches. My job was to pull chickens out of the cage and carry them to a dock where a truck waited to receive them. I wasn't sure where they went from there.

Anyway, it was and still is the hardest job I have ever had. Here is how it worked. We pulled chickens out of the cage and carried them about fifty feet to the end of the dock. Now picture about ten rows each with one person working a row. In the morning before we arrived at the ranch, we were picked up at a location, and on one day, I met an elderly man and his wife, a nice couple who looked as though they had spent a lifetime just trying to survive. You know those couples. For us they are an inspiration.

Well, each chicken can weigh a few pounds, and understand, they don't come out of the cage without a fight. And after a couple of minutes, you feel the pain of scratches and weight on your arms. The old man's wife would wait on the side of the ranch for the breaks we would get. Each break, she would have a nice little meal ready for her man, and they would invite me to sit and eat with them. Somehow she always had a little extra for me. This went on for a couple of weeks. One day, the old man had a pain on the side of his body and could not keep up. I remember on our first break I told him that we would work as a team. He would pull the chickens out and I would run them back to the dock. With a smile, he agreed. As I turned to his wife, there were tears in her face. After that day, I never saw them again...

Back to 2007 and the eyes of the old woman. You may not believe me, but some thirty-eight years later, they were the same eyes from the chicken ranch. Was this an angel giving me the opportunity to serve, or was this a test? Could be.

Sometimes it just takes a simple look into someone's eyes to change your life. When you look into the eyes, you have to answer. When the two women looked into my eyes back in school, they saw hope, and they answered with cookies. It was hope that built this country, and it is hope that will lead you and your family to a better tomorrow. My job is to touch as many people with hope as I can one at a time or by the thousands. It doesn't matter, and you can do the same.

This past Christmas, at a small park in Southern California, my family and some friends had a Christmas party for a group of about two thousand individuals where every kid received a new beautifully wrapped gift. Around one thousand were given out. We fed everyone hot dogs and chili beans, gave away fifty brand new bikes, about eighty free haircuts, and hundreds of boxes of food. Nothing was old, and everything was brand new. My mission: if it's not good enough for my kids, it's not good enough for any kids. My wife, three sons, two daughters-in-law, and five grandkids all helped serve at the event.

When my oldest son was about fourteen years old, I used to take him with me to feed the homeless. He did not realize how much it would impact his life and leadership skills. Years into the future, he is raising his family (one girl and two boys, and the girl is the oldest). One day after Thanksgiving, his daughter, my first granddaughter, told her parents at the age of five, "Let's take the leftover turkey and make sandwiches for the homeless." And today, the rest is history.

Again, when you look into the eyes of children and people of all ages, you will see the need, and it's time we get back to serving each other with dignity and hope. I can still see Santa back in 1965 in my old neighborhood sitting on top of the fire truck racing down the streets, siren bursting. Wow, Santa in my hood. Firemen, thank you for going beyond and bringing hope. We know that if you're in the room, all is well.

BIGGER
DOESN'T MEAN
BETTER

O n of the smartest executives I know one day
invited me to travel with him to visit some customers. On the plane, he asked me a career question about two positions that were open. One was huge with
a huge budget, and the other was small with a small budget.
Of course, I wanted the big job, until he began to describe
the other position and how I would fit the need. He actually
called me the chief encouragement officer—powerful words
from a great leader. Remember the old proverb that says life
and death are in the power of the tongue. These few simple
words spoke power and life to me. In my own mind, I sat
there for a moment and saw myself as the CEO of PepsiCo…
only I was the "chief encouragement officer. My job would be
to encourage everyone I came in contact with. The position
would mean working with the community of nonprofits. I
took the job and found myself enjoying one of the most ful-
filling times of my career. Eventually, the big job went away,
and my small job was replicated across the country, creating
many jobs! The reality is that there is no actual position like

this. The title of CEO is reserved for the top management individual of a company or organization, but maybe its time to add a Cheif Encouragement Officer as well!

———————

During the week, when my mother was not cleaning hotel rooms, she would work at one of the local fruit packing factories. The one she worked at packed oranges. It was called the Upland Packing House, and I always wondered why they called it a house when it was a factory. She worked the night shift and would get home around 11:00 p.m., but every night, she would bring home a couple of the biggest oranges anyone had ever seen. Most people will never see an orange as big as I did. At the end of each shift, the workers were allowed to take home a couple of oranges each. My mom always brought home the biggest. Some were the size of a small watermelon or bigger than a regular melon. What I noticed about the big oranges was that its peel was about an inch thick, and they were never sweet and always dry. One day I realized that the smaller oranges actually tasted better than the big ones, yet they were harder to peel than the larger ones.

If you have ever picked fruit, you will know that every tree has low-hanging fruit, but the sweetest is always at the top and on a limb. A fruit-bearing tree often contains some branches low enough for animals and humans to reach without much effort. The fruit contained on these lower branches may not be as ripe or attractive as the fruit on higher limbs, but it is usually more abundant and easier to harvest. From this we get the expression "low-hanging fruit," which means selecting the easiest fruit with the least amount of effort. Sounds good—except most times the easy things are not the great things.

In the case of fruit, if it is hanging low, it may be bruised or damaged by bugs or worms or animals, and it is also less likely to be ripe. Being experienced fruit pickers, we would always start at the top of a tree, where the fruit was more ready to eat because of greater exposure to the sun. And because as pickers we placed fruit in a bag over our shoulders, the bag got heavier as the job progressed, and starting at the top helped the pickers as they worked their way down.

Not all trees are the same. In an apple orchard, there may be different types of apples. Some are appealing and perfect for eating immediately but have a short life span. Others are better for shipping long distances, and still others are best for canning. Again, most fruit pickers understand that there needs to be a separation of fruit.

Will Rogers knew a little about picking fruit: "Why not go out on a limb? That's where the fruit is."

During the summers growing up, I loved staying at my grandmother's house. It was the only place on this earth where I was the main attraction. Nothing was like grandma's house. There was food until you would burst. I never told Grandma that there was nothing to eat; it was like a challenge. The adventure for me was in getting there. Grandma lived about ten miles from my home. But it was worth it; the ten miles was really nothing for a young traveler like me. My experience on riding the railroad cars from one town to the other was a great and cheap way to travel. You see, there were certain places about a mile from my house where the train would stop or come to a slow speed where one could run alongside and jump on board. I could ride it for a couple of miles and then walk the rest of the way. This was my daily taxi.

Between my mom and grandma, we would never go hungry. You know, when you think about it, it might be time to let a woman lead this country. I am sure she would do great, and there are two things I do know: she would make sure everyone had a roof over their head and food on the table. No one in the country would go without the basic needs of life. Women are great leaders. Their survival instincts include others; they are like captains of a ship—everyone else comes first.

After spending the day at Grandma's house, I would walk home in the early afternoon, and those of you from the sixties can remember we could walk for miles without any money, as there would be some fruit tree we could pick from or a Pepsi bottle to redeem for a nickel. Once I hit the jackpot on my way home. I decided to walk down our main street. Like many towns in those days, all the businesses and shops were located in a row on both sides of the street. This day, I passed a certain bank, and I looked in the window. To my amazement, there on a table in plain view was a table full of cookies and lemonade. Wow, for a starving kid, it was like walking into the land of milk and honey. Only for me, it was better, a land full of cookies and lemonade. For the next three days, I would walk in and grab a cup of lemonade and a handful of cookies. And like a great adventure, it became my oasis and the fuel that would get me home. This was until one dreadful day, the fourth day, as I walked in, I was greeted by the bank manager, who stopped me and told me to put the cookies back, as they were for the customers. You know, putting the cookies back really didn't hurt that badly, and he was right; they were for customers. It was clear I was not. What really did hurt though was the look in his eyes. I will never forget it; it was a look of complete disgust. But listen. That experience for me has led me to a place where I want to help feed every hungry child in the world and do it with a smile.

That bank was actually the biggest bank in the city. After it closed and went bankrupt, my first ever bank deposit went to the smallest bank in the town! Bigger is not always better.

Once you have tasted flight, you will forever walk the earth with your eyes turned skyward, for there you have been, and there you will always long to return.

—Leonard da Vinci

PHARAOH OR DELIVERER

There are many types of leaders, but I believe leadership boils down to two approaches: Pharaoh or a Deliverer.

A Pharaoh is one who takes captives and holds them by force. Their style is "serve me first," and they make it impossible for any of their people to experience growth.

A Deliverer is one who brings a message of freedom and growth to all who can hear. Their strategy is to serve others first.

We take for granted certain professions that because of title may automatically be labeled in a category of Pharaoh or Deliverer. But title and leadership style don't necessarily line up. If your profession is a jailer, one might think you fit in on the Pharaoh side; by the same token, a minister may be looked at as a Deliverer. But in reality, you can't place positions and titles together.

Leadership is not a title or position; it's a person with a spirit—a spirit to win as one. Coaches that win championships understand this spirit. They recognize that every person can and will contribute some sort of value. We all have the capacity to lead. No one is born a leader but we are all born to lead, born to lead something or someone.

Listen to the words of the most famous Deliverer spoken several thousands of years ago, "Let the people go," which set the people free to move in the direction they were intended to move in. So, CEOs–let the front line lead, ministers–let the congregation lead, legislature–follow the lead of your constituents and let their votes lead.

MANAGEMENT/PHARAOH VS. EMPOWERMENT/DELIVERER

"A battered horse named Seabiscuit, along with his owner, Charles Howard, a self made San Francisco businessman, Johnny "Red" Pollard, a down on his luck prize fighter turned jockey and a little known trainer named Tom Smith embodied the American spirit and gave hope to millions of Americans during the darkest economic era our nation has ever faced. With the help of these three men and one victory after another Seabiscuit lifted the citizens of our country out of the despair of the Great Depression. In 1938, he became the greatest icon of his time garnering more press than President Franklin D. Roosevelt." [3]

Sea Biscuit, at first glance, was not much to look at and certainly did not have the look of a champion. Having lost his first few races, almost everyone gave up on him until a few took the second glance and something stood out. I am not sure what that that one thing was, but those who took the second look knew. They saw something others could not, a champion. Take that same horse, add a new trainer...and history is made. Great leaders do the same. They take a second look at people, even those who may not have the look of champions, and bring with them new ways of leading and, in most cases, they just let you run!

You see, Deliverers lead with optimism – the spirit that believes they can do something to change this situation for the better.

You may not look like a champion, but those leaders can see value where others can't. Once these electrifying leaders come into your life with their sometimes *crazy* methods of training and empowerment, you are left never-the-same!

What you expect from life is not the same as what life expects from you. When you move forward the country moves forward. You may be like many of us—not much to look at and maybe you've lost your first few races. Optimism can change all that and you can become like Sea Biscuit with an electrifying energy that, combined with your speed and fighting spirit, rallies your family or organization to your greatest year, despite what the economy says.

Merriam Webster's definition of electrify: to charge with electricity, to equip for use of electric power, to supply with power, to amplify, to excite intensely or suddenly

Synonyms: charge, thrill, excite, exhilarate, galvanize, intoxicate, pump up, titillate, turn on".

The starting gate is open, run your race!

Let me make it personal. As you may recall I mentioned a few chapters back that when I took the class given by the community minister, he gave me an A on my first test—my first A, ever. What I didn't mention was how I turned in the report. Understand that I had no knowledge of what school was all about. So when it came time to turn in our reports, I remember writing it out on regular paper, then my creativity began to move in, and I took some old newspaper and created my own binder, then I took all three pages and taped them together to look like my version of what a report should look like. You see, this leader, the minister, was a Deliverer and with this A he set me free from all the past incidents that would have held me down to a level that none of us are destined for. In a sense, he broke the chains that would have kept me captive to ignorance of intelligence, and he helped release the brilliance of my life that would follow.

"IT'S OUR THEME THAT LEADS US TO OUR DREAMS"

Nowhere is optimism more important than while leading an organization. Highly effective leaders have a transforming effect on their constituents. They have the gift of being able to convince others that they can achieve levels of performance beyond what they thought possible. Remember greatness is not governed by reality—reality is governed by greatness, and when you become great you give others permission to also become great.

So you can find leadership at all levels of life. It's not just the most prestigious universities and their alumni that own the rights to leadership. As a matter of fact, I think it's time for many of them to examine what they teach and reward as leadership, because whatever our country is experiencing, good or bad, is always traced back to leadership. It's time for the government leaders to revisit how they see leadership. It's time for the board rooms of corporate America to revisit how they see leadership. It's time for the churches to revisit leadership. These three entities are the foundation of what made our country what is it today. It's time for you to let go and learn from the single parent of three trying to feed everyone on a income for two. We can learn from her, or the father who is volunteering to coach a sports team. The grandparents of the world know what true leadership is—its time to look at leadership from the hearts of the true front line leaders. People that care about people.

THERE ARE NO BAD KIDS, ONLY KIDS IN BAD ENVIRONMENTS

When I was about eight years old I had my first experience with the law. Back in school, I can remember the teacher walking across the room and circling the tables where she had placed us in groups of five per table. Our assignment was to draw and color anything we wanted. I can still see her face smiling saying, "Johnnie, that's nice. Mary, very beautiful. Sandy, how colorful." I was next and held my picture up so she couldn't miss it. I thought, maybe I could be the next class star, maybe the next to lead the Pledge of Allegiance, but I was stunned as she walked by without uttering a single word. My young mind didn't understand and I tried to analyze what had just happened. Then it hit me: was it my color? Is it possible that my dark skin was a negative force that would be a setback?

I thought I needed to find a way that could make her notice my pictures. I thought, "Hey I know, more colors! Colors no one else in the class room has." Well buying new crayons or markers was pretty much financially impossible for my family, as we barely had enough to pay for food and rent. So I headed to the nearby market that served the area. In hindsight, my actions were wrong but my desires for acceptance were stronger. You guessed it; I stole package of markers, apparently I was not a good thief because as I walked out of the store, standing there waiting for me was the manager. He quickly stopped me, found the markers in my pocket, took me back in the store and called the police. I was arrested placed in back of the police car with my bike in his trunk. I can still hear his voice as he spoke with the others on his police radio. "You guys will never believe what I have in the car! An 8-year-old thief." And it got worse. Instead of taking me into the station he released me to my Mom. As we pulled up to our house, there she was talking to the other neighborhood women. I will never forget the sadness in her eyes when she saw her firstborn son sitting in the rear seat of the police car. That night the hurt in the eyes of my parents was worse than the other punishment I received. (Well no, it's was more like *even*!)

For me, that day impacted my future because the other moms would not allow their children to play or associate with me. It's one thing to be rejected by others but to be rejected by your own is almost impossible to overcome without some type of supernatural intervention. Now I was not only dark on the outside, I was now also dark on the inside. But it never felt right because my heart was full of love. I loved everyone. This was the first time in my life that I heard the small inner voice that would never leave me, even when the entire world seemed to. This was the voice that would be my counsel many times, the same small voice that speaks to you. The voice that said, "Richard, someday you will lead thousands of children and help them reach their destiny." What's interesting is that the small voice is bilingual it speaks in the language you understand. I heard it in Spanish and English.

> "You plant the same seed on both sides of that wall. On one side, there is shade; the flower will not grow as tall. It will be stunted. On the other side, there is sunlight, and the flower grows tall from the same seed."
>
> —Rev. Jesse Jackson

I never intended in my heart to steal, and I make no excuses, but it's important to understand that today our children all need to have the best and equal supplies of opportunities, and many of us are in the perfect place to tear down the walls that block the sunlight. Empowering all our children is the best means of creating a common denominator for success. I finally found a way to right the wrong of 1963 by freely providing school supplies for thousands of kids every year since 2003.

Our prisons walls are filled with men and women who at one time were just innocent kids, and I have since realized that there are no bad kids, only kids in bad environments.

Another favorite quote goes something like this, "and I will give you treasures out of darkness." You have an opportunity to take all the dark moments of your life and turn them into treasures.

The word treasure has roots from the Greek *thēsauros*, meaning "treasure store and a concentration of riches, often one which is considered lost or forgotten until being rediscovered." You see, we can rediscover the treasures of our life that were once lost!

Doing the right thing will take off your hand cuffs and exchange them for cuff links. The right thing will take off your prison jumpsuit and exchange it for a blue business suit. The right thing will take you from the prison floors, to the palace floors. Save a child and we save our world!

UNDERSTAND ME... BEFORE YOU TRY TO RESHAPE ME!

One of the most fascinating pictures I have seen is the illusion of a frog and horse, not sure who created the image. First time I saw it, my mind raced with such great emotions and I thought, *wow one picture with two illusions.* How did the artist see it?

The human brain is a complex organ responsible for intelligence, senses, movement, and behavior. The halves of the brain—the "right brain" and the "left brain"—perform different functions and communicate information with each other through a band of nerves that connect them. The right side of the brain controls most of the movement and functions of the left side of the body and the left side of the brain controls most of the movements and functions of the right side of the body.

You may hear that someone is a "right-brained" or "left-brained" individual. This is called "brain dominance," meaning that an individual has a natural preference for processing information on one side of the brain. The right side is considered the intuitive or spontaneous side, while the left side is logical. Knowing an individual's brain dominance can help you understand his/her "ways" of thinking, behaving, speaking, and functioning. Also, it can help parents and educators understand a child's natural learning preferences. Right-brain characteristics include creativity, the ability to see patterns, and the understanding of how things relate to one another in different contexts. You may find that these individuals seem to have "out-of-the-box" ideas and talents including the ability to draw, paint, and sculpt, think imaginatively, and even musical talents, including the ability to play instruments. Left-brain characteristics include a gift for language, analytical skills, and mathematical concepts such as time and sequence. You may find that individuals with this brain dominance are good with letters, numbers, and words. These individuals seem to "have a natural gift for" language skills including reading, writing, and speaking math, science.

Now Some experts believe that its not really possible to function at a high level on both sides of the brain, that there is always a dominate side leading. This might be true but in my experience as a self proclaimed expert, with a PhD on being Poor Hungry and Determined, and just someone who, like you, refuses to accept theory that places limitations on my abilities. Look at the construction worker and the carpenter. They both use creativity and calculations when building or repairing something. He or she first sees it in their mind (right side) then sends it to the left side and then they pull out their measuring tapes and very sophisticated tools. We have some of the worlds greatest minds working on paving our roads and building our schools yet you will never hear of them, and just because we don't hear of them does not mean they don't exist. It was both left and right brain that built this country and it will be the same that holds us together.

One of the greatest minds of all time, Leonardo da Vinci, once said that he did not know if he was a scientist who loves to study the Arts or an Artist that loves to study the Science, either way he studies both.

WHAT IS MORE IMPORTANT TO THINK OR TO LEARN?

Someone said, "Only when you consider your failure to be final, you're finally a failure." Look, failure is not a situation, only an opinion, and as long as it's not your opinion you can come back and succeed. The person who doesn't make mistakes is unlikely to make anything.

Look at how the eye functions…

It is true that the images formed on your retina are up-side-down. Processing visual information is a complex task that takes up a relatively large portion of the brain compared to other senses. This is because your brain performs several tasks to make images 'easier' to see. One part is handled in the optic part of your brain itself, and part of its job is to make images right-side-up. It does this because your brain is so used to seeing things upside-down that it eventually adjusts to it. A few leaders can see both upside and down. It was a leader who saw the benefit in taking a company and turning it upside down and running it that way; meaning those closest to the customer and product would be the most critical employees and those at HQ would be their to support the front line. This is a bold strategy for any company, a strategy our legislators can learn from, and what is important to the people you serve!

We need to understand how to develop and use the education we have been given in order to not become victims. Here's what I mean: education may teach you that a square peg won't fit in a round hole. You can make it fit the question is why would you want to. Listen CEO, Teacher, Parent: we all have a shape and a destiny. In other words, no matter what shape you were created in; you have a place to fit. You start your life as a square peg or round hole in a world that is in conflict with its shapes (this why diversity is so important to our nation for future survival). The first thing we learn in school, well not sure I learned it but I did see it, everyone stop talking, stand in line quietly, and the kids who had a struggle with always talking and not able to stand in one spot for more than two minutes were constantly in some type of trouble. This is where the different shapes begin to label a child based on their respective shape...wow how wrong is this. Listen, I understand our kids need rules, that's not what I am talking about, what I am trying to say is just because you can't see the kid's greatness and uniqueness does not mean they are not more than capable of developing into high productive leaders. We should never try to reshape a child's look or to form our identity on them. What we should do is help the child shape their God given identity into a productive person and human being.

Our creator, whoever you may call him or her, a supreme being or nature, no one is created without a specific purpose or as a mistake. Many times I look back and wonder what my life would have been had someone seen me in the shape I was meant to be. We usually don't like people who do not follow the rules, but without them nothing would change, as it is the rule breakers that motivate society to change its rules. It was a rule breaker that discovered the world was not actually flat. It was a rule breaker who had a dream of America as a place of freedom for all individuals. It was a rule breaker who said front line workers can contribute as much as executives. So if you are a shape trying to fit into a place not fitted for you and it works great, and then by all means go for it. But if you're the shape that is having problems finding the fit. Give up the struggle and release the shape you were created in and accept the fact you may never fit in and that's okay.

Many will expect you to live within their own shape or limitations. "I'm the boss here and this is how we do it," "Because I'm the teacher and I know more," (really I'm sure some of you do, but how many of you know what's its like to spend the day looking for your next meal, you find ways to educate yourself for survival.) Look, there are parts of my past that I don't like to talk about, but I needed to survive and I found ways.

I remember saving soda pop bottles, since back in my days a 5 cent return was a great deal of change. Collect 10 bottles and you have 50 cents! You know what we could buy back then? Well, one example of using my creative side was walking across the tracks to the other side of town and knocking on the homes of the rich. I'd negotiate a good price to purchase their soda pop bottles at. Many times the rich would simply let me take the bottles; you know the rich are usually generous they just need a cause to invest in. By the end of the day I could have as much as a $1.50. Now the part you don't want to mention to your kids is that I did this during school hours, but for me as a ten year old boy eating was more important that learning. A buck fifty could buy some good bologna and bread, and of course some Fritos and Pepsi.

During this time in my life there were many who were trying to reshape me instead of trying to understand me. I know the majority of them had the right intentions and to-day I still appreciate those people that help keep our kids in school. I wish we could be like our military forces, "No Solider Left Behind"—No kid left behind.

The truant officers would many times pick me up and take me right back to school. I remember as they dropped me off I would walk straight through the front of the school and cross the entire yard and walk right out the other end. You can try to fit in or you can escape and follow your destiny. After several of these encounters, society said enough and I landed behind bars at age 12 for not going to school. Today, I still don't understand why I was locked up for just wanting to work. After many months locked in a cell, the Judge re-leased me. It would be like that my entire youth until I turned 18, when by law I was no longer required to attend school. I know the system was there to try and help me, but maybe it's time to change the system. Maybe we can't change the systems of the world but we can at the very least change our personal systems and treat every child in the world as our own!

By the time you are old enough to understand your own mind, you may find yourself many times in a place that wasn't created for you. A life that just doesn't seem to fit right. Some of us have been sold an idea of what someone else's opinions of us are, or again maybe you were told at a young age that you are inadequate for anything great; you're damaged goods. You are far removed from your destiny and life's purpose has eluded you. Well, not true. You are far from being damaged goods; you hold secrets within you just waiting to be set free. Secrets that only you can see, secrets that a special needs child can hold!

In the 70s, when recycling aluminum cans became popular, I became an advert collector and recycler, based not on my ecological concerns but more on my economic concerns. I needed the money but today I recycle based on taking care of our planet. What I am trying to get at is that while I was collecting cans my father invented the first aluminum can crusher. No he was not the first to patent it or sell it, but I will argue he was the first to invent it. Now here is a genius with a 3rd grade education that saw a need and the answer to the need. He built it with parts that were discarded in junk yards. It worked perfectly and today I still have that treasure. You see when my father saw me, he saw treasure. My question for you is can you see the treasure before you!

THE FIRST AND LAST

To have a servant's heart is one of the greatest gifts to this world.

Back in the 1960s, on one of my many nights sleeping in the park, I saw a gentleman about the age of 50 years old. The guy walked slowly as he approached, greeting me with a hello. I am not sure why I wasn't afraid of this total stranger. It was obvious he was homeless and he asked if he could sit for awhile and as a 12 year old adventurer I welcomed him to sit.

Our conversation began as small talk but soon grew into a life conversation between two friends! He began to tell me about his days serving in the military during Korea and Vietnam. His job was cleaning and washing tires. I asked him, "why tires?" and he responded, "Somebody had to do it, why not me?" And I guessed he was right. The next day he went on his way and I on mine and I could not help but feel a sense of sadness in my heart for him. Here was a man who served his country for many years with pride and yet it didn't seem right for him to be homeless. While I did not know what circumstance in his life lead to his situation, it didn't matter to me I just spent time with a hero.

I have had the privilege of standing on the corners of what is known as *the day laborers camp*. Men of all ages, young and old, tall and short, stand and wait for someone to pull up and announce "workers needed." But you know it's always the ones that look youngest and strongest that get picked first. At any time of the day you will see men waiting and hoping to be picked for work. As the day moves on men still wait, but it's always the same group that goes first. There is a story or parable about the first being last and the last being first. I never really understood what that meant until one day in 2008 I received an invitation along with a group of other business leaders across the country to meet with the president of the United States.

I was not quite sure how I got on the list as I was always the last to get picked for anything. The event took place on the Rose Garden grounds with a small luncheon. During the beginning of the event the president walked on to a small stage or platform to address the group for about fifteen minutes. There were about 40 business leaders CEOs and people of influence, yet I continued to wonder, how did I end up with this group? The seating was open, with no assigned seats. After the president took his place it was announced please take your seat, everyone ran to get the best seats in the house. The first row quickly filled and I found myself in a familiar place: the worst seat in the house. I could not see anything, and I thought, *Oh well, another missed opportunity.* But for some strange reason the small voice said to me, "The last shall be first and the first shall be last." I remember the old military veteran who I spent the night talking and listing to his stories and I remember what he said about his job cleaning tires—that somebody has to do it. I knew then that somebody had to sit in the worst seat in the house, so why not me. After the president spoke we were all escorted out by rows with the last row and seat being let out first. That was my seat, and being in that seat put me right in the path of the President, who greeted me personally, as he exited. As he reached out to shake my hand I brought him in and hugged him, and while I had him next to me, I whispered into his ear a message he needed to hear—a message sent from the back of the room, a message that placed a smile in his heart, a message that for a moment I know brought him great relief. So I have learned that the worst seats in the house can actually be the best. We can all learn from the movie, Forrest Gump. Just show up and see what happens.

SUCCESS DOESN'T CHANGE ANYONE... IT ONLY REVEALS THEM

A *breakout* is a military operation term meaning "to end a situation of encirclement or siege." A breakout is achieved when the encircled forces and its allies (perhaps from outside the encirclement) attack a weak point in the encirclement, creating a breakthrough, and then move through that gap to freedom. [4]

Innovation is the creation of better or more effective products, processes, services, and ideas that are accepted by society. Innovation differs from invention in that innovation refers to the use of a new idea or method, whereas invention refers more directly to the creation of the idea or method itself. The word *innovation* derives from the Latin word *innovatus*, which is the noun form of *innovare*, which means "to renew or change." I love the old French version, to go around as an innover, "one who makes and renews."

Technically, *innovation* is defined merely as "introducing something new." There are no qualifiers of how groundbreaking or world-shattering that something needs to be— only that it needs to be better than what was there before.

The fact is, innovation means different things to different people.

Innovation is the process through which value is created and delivered to a community of users in the form of a new solution. Creativity, by contrast, is the ability to imagine new concepts. It is important to understand that creativity does not carry the burden of value creation that innovation does. Here is a great example of one who broke out and became an innovator.

The first recorded woman to graduate from medical school in 1849, Elizabeth Blackwell, was the first female doctor in the United States and the first on the UK Medical Register, as well as a pioneer in educating women in medicine. On January 11, 1849, Blackwell became the first woman to achieve a medical degree in the United States and graduated on January 23, 1849.

Listen, she was banned from practice in most hospitals. She was advised to go to Paris, France, and train at La Maternité, but she had to continue her training as a student midwife, not as a physician. While she was there, her training was cut short when in November 1849 she caught a serious eye infection from a baby she was treating. She had to have her right eye removed and replaced with a glass eye. This loss brought to an end her hopes to become a surgeon.

In 1857, Blackwell, along with her sister, Emily, and another female doctor Dr. Marie Zakrzewska, founded their own infirmary, the New York Infirmary for Women and Children in a single-room dispensary near Tompkins Square in Manhattan. During the American Civil War, Blackwell trained many women to be nurses and sent them to the army.

After the war, Blackwell had time, in 1868, to establish a Women's Medical College at the infirmary to train women physicians and doctors.

We can learn from Dr. Blackwell and her passion for innovation and her courage to break out. She was willing to change.

One of the root words for *change* comes from the Greeks. In Greek mythology, Proteus is a sea god whose name suggests change, because he was able to change his shape as needed to escape capture. He could also foretell the future, but would change his shape to avoid having to do it; he would answer only to someone who was capable of capturing him. Because of this characteristic of Proteus also comes the word protean, with the general meaning of versatile, capable of assuming many forms with a positive meaning of flexibility, versatility and adaptability...In simple words, change is courage. Remember, like Proteus, change can keep you from being trapped. (wikipedia.com)

—————◆◦❈◦◆—————

Some of you may remember the S&H Green Stamps; they were trading stamps popular in the United States from the 1930s until the late 1980s. They were distributed as part of a rewards program operated by the Sperry and Hutchinson company (S&H) founded in 1896 by Thomas Sperry and Shelly Hutchinson. During the 1960s, the rewards catalog printed by the company was the largest publication in the United States, and the company issued three times as many stamps as the U.S. Postal Service. Customers would receive stamps at the checkout counter of supermarkets, department stores, and gasoline stations among other retailers, which could be redeemed for products in the catalog.

Sperry and Hutchinson began offering stamps to U.S. retailers in 1896. The retail organizations that distributed the stamps (primarily supermarkets, gasoline filling stations, and shops) bought the stamps from S&H and gave them as bonuses to shoppers based on the dollar amount of a purchase. The stamps were issued in denominations of one, ten, and fifty "points," and as shoppers accumulated the stamps, they placed them in collectors' books, which were provided free by S&H. The books contained twenty-four pages, and to fill a page, a shopper needed fifty "points," so each book contained 1,200 "points." Shoppers could then exchange filled books for premiums, including house wares and other items, from the local Green Stamps store or catalog.

For us as a family, it meant more than just a free gift; it meant we could own something we never would purchase with actual money, something that we would consider extravagant, like a blender or maybe a vacuum cleaner for Mom. And in our neighborhood, we had the choice of selling our completed books to one of the local wealthy persons on the other side of the tracks, who would buy the books from us for $1.25 a book. Many times, these stamps kept us from starving. As a ten-year-old, I did pretty well in my negotiations, as the man I was selling to would always try to bring the price down to an even dollar. It was not my math skills that helped me with the negotiations; it was the hunger of a family full of kids. These are the types of innovations we need today, innovations from which we all can benefit.

Remember, innovation is simply making something better, a gift we can all give!

As leaders, we need to understand that people are moved and inspired by passion, and how they see your life is a reflection of how they will follow you.

Nothing in the universe is stagnant. It is either expanding or contracting. Life is either in the process of becoming or in the process of dying. Scientists use the term *entropy* to describe things that come to an end. When something is actively becoming more, they say it is antip-entropic. It is impossible for you to stay the same. You are either growing yourself, or you are in the process of becoming less.

When you are inspired by a great purpose, everything will begin to work for you.

There have been certain inspired breakthroughs in the world that have changed the course of history: electricity, the automobile, and the telephone to name just a few. If these seeds of innovation were never planted and released, our lives would not be as they are today.

One of the greatest tragedies in nature is the waste of a seed or the isolation of a seed from soil. It seems terrible that we keep seeds from reaching their intended destiny!

I remember back in the sixties standing in line with my mom to receive our government-assisted food every two weeks. This was before food stamps were around. It was more like a food bank—not bad food; we enjoyed it. For us kids, it was the same as going grocery shopping, but for my mom and dad, it never really seemed like a good time. It was not until I was older that I realized why they felt that way. Many times society will frown on those on the receiving end of government-assistance programs. I know that there is a controversy on this subject, and I am not here to debate it. What I do want others to know is that standing in that line is difficult to do. One day, I decided never to stand in that line again. Somehow, we would make it. Well, we struggled without it, but we found ways to make it. My father worked two jobs, and my mom worked one job and one part-time on the weekends. She, with one of my younger sisters, would clean motel rooms for a couple of dollars per room.

That's when a seed in me began to germinate, a seed that someday would lead me to feed thousands of families, feeding them with dignity. And today, we have taken thousands of groceries to families in need across the country and of course in my hometown. Government agencies began to call on me for help. The one who needed help is now in a position to help. Sometimes you just need to know that whatever you experienced—good or bad—in life, if you take it and allow it to be used, it can turn into something great.

The ultimate contrast between those who are successful and those who are not is not in anything on the outside or experience, its within your spirit and zeal. You see, zeal uses the ordinary unexpected, ordinary unimpressive, and the ordinary inexperienced to accomplish extraordinary things. Zeal keeps you going when others quit. It pushes you through the toughest times and gives you energy you didn't know you possessed. Add enthusiasm to your game and you can't lose. *Enthusiasm* comes from the Greek word *enthous*, meaning possessed by a god or large spirit within, or to be inspired by a god.

Born into poverty, hard times, or with little formal education can make the journey more difficult but with the right attitude you can also take the negatives and make positives. You see, for me I finally realized it's all the past negatives in my life that have and are leading me today to all the positives in my life.

Remember every person can choose to lead but the one who leads with enthusiasm inspires others and can be the one that will change, provide a vision for the future, and also offer encouragement to others to achieve. We may never be the best player on the team, but we can be the best player for the team!

It was my passion for leading people that led to results. Listen. Always remember: we drive cattle, but we lead people. When you see the needs, your seeds come alive, and sometimes, we just need leaders who know how to survive. I don't care if you got an A in economics, and I don't care if you quit school at a young age. What we care about is if you can lead us beyond the path of survival into the land of milk and honey.

It doesn't matter how old the seed is. Take a look at this story from National Geographic:

The oldest plant ever to be regenerated has been grown from 32,000-year-old seeds—beating the previous record holder by some 30,000 years.

A Russian team discovered a seed cache of Silene stenophylla, a flowering plant native to Siberia, that had been buried by an Ice Age squirrel near the banks of the Kolyma River . Radiocarbon dating confirmed that the seeds were 32,000 years old.

The mature and immature seeds, which had been entirely encased in ice, were unearthed from

124 feet below the permafrost, surrounded by layers that included mammoth, bison, and woolly rhinoceros bones.

The mature seeds had been damaged—perhaps by the squirrel itself, to prevent them from germinating in the burrow. But some of the immature seeds retained viable plant material.

The team extracted that tissue from the frozen seeds, placed it in vials, and successfully germinated the plants, according to a new study. The plants—identical to each other but with different flower shapes from modern S. stenophylla—grew, flowered, and, after a year, created seeds of their own. [5]

Everything in creation is designed to function on the simple principle of receiving and releasing. Life depends on this principle. Plants release oxygen. People release encouragement.

Again, it doesn't matter how old the seed is; it never dies. What was deposited in you can live again.

The tremendous seeds you and I have been given are locked inside us waiting to be germinated. We owe it to the next generation to live with courage so that the treasures of our potential are unleashed. The world needs what has been deposited in us. We are obligated to release to the world.

With every ability comes a responsibility, a responsibility that every person is born with seeds.

One of the most misunderstood words in modern English is *meek*. Meekness is commonly defined as a deficiency in spirit and courage. Meekness is not a synonym for weakness. To be meek doesn't mean to be spineless and cowardly.

Here's what meekness means: The original word *meek* comes from the Greek word *praos*. It means to be "mild, humble, and gentle." But the Greeks also used the word *praos* to describe the process of taming an animal, such as a wild horse. When a wild horse is broken and trained, its power is harnessed and brought under control. This puts meekness as a person whose power, strength, and ability are brought under control and used in a positive way.

A meek person is really a special gift and yet one of the most resisted gifts. Meekness is power under control. Meekness is never to be confused with weakness. Weakness is the absence of strength and power, meekness is possessing strength and power, yet restraining oneself from using it choosing to be meek for graceful purposes.

The Greeks also used the word to describe a soothing medicine, a gentle breeze, or a domesticated colt...Power under control.

Meekness is not the absence of fear, it's the conquest of it.

I never knew Sam Walton of Walmart, but I do know that his success put him in a position to give back to the community. They are today one of the leaders in giving back to community. My mom loves Walmart. With several dozen grandkids and great-grandkids, she can always find a great, affordable gift for all occasions.

George Draper Dayton was a founder of Target stores. While Dayton had a desire to become a minister, he fell in love with the business world. It's interesting to see that Dayton's heart was to be a minister. What he accomplished in his life was nothing short of a minister. In a certain sense, he is a model for ministers to follow. Like many of you, he was a living and walking example of servant leadership before it was a book. In 1883, he moved to Worthington, Minnesota, with his family and was dedicated to giving back to his community. He was heavily involved with the Worthington Board of Education, as well as his church community.

In 1902, he founded Dayton's Dry Goods store in Minneapolis, which eventually became Dayton's department store. As his success as a businessman grew, Dayton's dedication to service continued, as he gave back to his church as well as established the Dayton Foundation, one of the first foundations of its kind in corporate America. You see, Mr. Dayton was great not because of his wealth; it was what he did with it that made him great.

Barney Kroger, who founded the Kroger chain of supermarkets, was born in Cincinnati, Ohio, in a family of German immigrants. Kroger went to work at age thirteen to support his family, and after working in a drug store, as a farmhand, and as a door-to-door salesman, he established the stores that would eventually became known simply as Kroger.

Amid his success, Kroger, like Dayton, contributed to many worthy causes, including the development of parks and zoos, while donating to medical research projects. He was another great leader who knew his responsibility to others.

Women have such a unique ability too energize people. They are like generators. Here is the description of the word *generator* from many dictionaries: Generator– a machine that converts mechanical energy into electricity to serve as a power source for other machines. A generator is someone who originates or initiates something, "she was the generator of several ideas." The root word in Latin *generare* means "to produce" or "to bring into being, a process of creating." In simple terms a generator is a machine that converts mechanical energy into electrical energy.

Listen, like electrical generators that feed other machines, great leaders have the ability to generate positive energy. They are "people generators" and they carry energy for others to pull from. They are family members or coworkers, and when they walk into the room the entire room is lit up with positive energy.

One of the most powerful ways to increase your energy is to shift your focus to the generator you carry within you. Everything you will ever need for success is already within you…Just hit the switch.

Within PepsiCo, you will find some of the world's brilliant female minds from the CEO to the front line—women who have inspired me with their abilities to innovate and lead. I have always believed that when God created women, he was truly innovating!

There are many stories of people, even today, who started selling produce or burritos on the side of the road, and today those road carts are billion-dollar organizations. I am positive that if you search their organizations, you will find that they are also some of the biggest givers back to the community.

For me, much of my energy comes from the special women in my life: my wife, who never stops believing in me; my mom who never had much, but somehow she found a way to give much; my mother-in-law, in whose eyes I can do no wrong; my two daughters-in-law, who add sweet and spice to the Montañez family and bring the heart of serving others; my two granddaughters who remind me of how good it feels to be loved. And then there are the men in my family: my three sons, who are destined for greatness, and my three grandsons, future servant leaders!

BIBLIOGRAPHY

1   Munroe, Dr. Myles, *The Principles and Power of Vision*, Whitaker House, 2003.

2   Williamson, Marianne, *A Return to Love: Reflections on the Principles of "A Course in Miracles,"* Harper Paperbacks; Reissue Edition, March 15, 1996.

3   *The Heartwarming Story of Seabiscuit,* http://www.seabiscuitheritage.org

4   http://en.wikipedia.org/wiki/Breakout_(military)

5   Rachel Kaufman, *32,000-Year-Old Plant Brought Back to Life—Oldest Yet,* National Geographic News, http://news.nationalgeographic.com/news/2012/02/120221-oldest-seeds-regenerated-plants-science/, Feb. 21, 2012.

CPSIA information can be obtained at www.ICGtesting.com
Printed in the USA
LVOW04s0236260315

432087LV00024B/423/P